C000046611

NOT EVEN
A NUMBER

Surviving Lager C ~ Auschwitz II-Birkenau

Edith Perl

and

Lindsay Preston

M⊙tivational PRESS
LEADERS IN GLOBAL PUBLISHING

Published by Motivational Press, Inc.
1777 Aurora Road
Melbourne, Florida, 32935
www.MotivationalPress.com

Manufactured in the United States of America.

ISBN: 978-1-62865-362-5

CONTENTS

Thank you to Susan and Hallie for all of your help.

DEDICATION

THIS BOOK IS DEDICATED TO my Momma Ruzena (Rose) Grosman Kalus, to my brothers and sister, Yidel, Pearl, and Mendel, who died the day we arrived to Auschwitz II- Birkeneu, and to my brave, little sister Goldie who died in the gas chambers after suffering for six and a half months.

My Momma had pushed Goldie, Joli and I across the train tracks to life, entreating me to stay alive and entrusting me to protect my sisters. She told me to endure so I could tell our story, to make sure that the millions who died at the hands of Adolf Hitler and the Nazi's would not be forgotten.

Now, after 70 years, I am telling the story just as my Momma wanted me to.

INTRODUCTION

MEMORIES ARE A FASCINATING THING. The flickering of a face in the crowd, a child's laugh, a familiar smell can spur a lifetime of recollections. As I get older, the flashes of my childhood come to me more often and more vividly. The sight of the Shabbat candles glowing on the Sabbath brings back my Momma's prayers for health and wellbeing. Men with bushy mustaches remind me of my Papa's fuzzy kisses. I look at my ninety-year-old self and think of my Grandma and remember how her skin felt when I scratched her back. I can't help but laugh now as my skin rolls and tumbles under my hands.

At this point in my life, I try not to dwell on the sad days of the German occupation of Czechoslovakia and my months as a prisoner of the Nazis but the memories flood my mind at the oddest times and still all these years later I am brought to tears. I remember crying on my forty-second birthday, the age my Momma was when she died in the gas chambers. I remember feeling so alive, like I could jump across buildings and her life had ended so abruptly. I cried when my children turned eleven, the age my little Goldie died. Tiny things would remind me of all that I had lost and then I need to remind myself that I am a survivor.

My name is Edith Perl, but in my lifetime I have been known by many names: my grandma called me Sura Rifka, my Papa, brothers and sisters called me Rifchu. My Momma, who hated my given name, called me "Blondie" or "her big girl." During my time in the camp my name was Edita. To the Nazis I was just a body, a useless thing that wasn't even worth a number.

CHAPTER ONE

HOME

T HE SUN SET A PERFECT glow over the rolling hills and lush valleys. Green grass and colored wild flowers covered the hills and plains. At the lowest point flowed the Latorica River. This rapidly running river winded its way around Sub-Carpathia, the far eastern province of Czechlosovakia.

On the outskirts of the Sub-Carpathian Mountains, at the edge of the tiny town of Vlachovice was a small village, this was where I lived. There were less than thirty families in our village with nothing more than a dirt path connecting us, and sometimes less than that.

My parents, my eight brothers and sisters and my grandma and I lived a comfortable life on a farm and small onsite mill with a large waterwheel that helped to produce the flour and grain. I loved our waterwheel. I loved listening to it at night, the water pressure collapsing paddle over paddle. I loved my home.

My Papa ran the lumber business and my Momma worked at the mill that was attached to our house. My Momma had taught me how to make flour in the mill and also to do all of the duties a girl should do around the house. "I was the oldest daughter." The one she relied on and I was more than obliged to be her right hand. I would follow her around every day during the summer cleaning, cooking, gardening, and tending the mill. I had the routine down so well that I knew what my mother was going to do or say even before she did. The only time I would leave her side was when the Drummer came to town. When the Drummer came to town, I would act every bit my young age. I didn't care what Momma needed handled or how many younger kids were hanging on her.

When I heard the banging of the drum in the distance, I would rush like a whirlwind past my Momma who was tending the garden. But she knew me just as well, and without even looking up from the earth, Momma would yell, "Take your sisters!"

So, on the very hot and steamy August day when I heard the banging in the distance and I started to run off I was stopped by my Momma, "Not so fast, Blondie. Wait for Joli and Goldie."

"I'm in a hurry, Momma," I yelled back.

"You can wait," Momma yelled amidst the flowers and tomatoes, her body bobbing as she worked. I wanted to protest, but I never did. That was not how Momma raised me. So, like I did every time, I waited by, the garden fence for my younger sisters Joli and Goldie to join me for the walk into town. I tapped my foot impatiently.

"Joli, Goldie, hurry up! The Drummer won't wait for us!" I called up towards the house.

"Have some patience, child," Momma chirped to me.

I crossed my hands in a huff. I understood that I had to wait for my sisters but I didn't understand that I had to like it.

"Baby girl, I want you to uncross those arms!" Momma said, "You don't have to show the world how you feel. Be stronger than that."

I dropped my arms in a huff. Finally, my sisters came out.

"Be good. Hold Goldie's hand. Don't let Joli out of your sight. No running. Be home before dark. Be respectable to those around you. Do you hear me girls?" Momma asked.

"Yes, Momma," we would say in unison.

We took off walking down the dirt path hand in hand. Once we knew we were out of Momma's sight we would drop hands and start running, the dust flying behind us.

When I was Goldie's age, Momma would take me to the square to hear the Drummer announce the news. I never understood what he was talking about but I loved the excitement, the crowd, and the way the Drummer announced the news.

The Drummer was an old man now. His body was thin and his face was long and pointy like the rats that ran around our barn. His dark bulging eyes would study the crowd. It had been almost ten years since I had first come with Momma to see the drummer and his routine had never varied: first he took out his pipe, packed it, and lit it. He puffed and waited till the stragglers arrived. In the summertime, he might push his straw hat back off his forehead, take out a handkerchief and wipe his brow. In the winter he would rub his hands together and stamp his feet in the snow. We knew the preliminaries were over when the Drummer spat on the ground; sometimes in winter he would spit and it would splatter black over the white snow. After he spit and banged on his drum on more time, he ceremoniously removed a long sheet of paper out of his pouch. For all that show, the news was rarely extraordinary.

We waited for the Drummer to speak. He wiped his brow, "A band of gypsies are passing through the area. Coyotes are killing the livestock just outside of town – keep a watchful eye. There will be a town meeting next week to discuss next year's taxes." When it was over, the Drummer spat again and headed for the tavern.

While the news was never too exciting, the event of going into town was. Everyone was so friendly and happy. There was always some adult there handing out candy to the kids, which was a real treat for us. We would run around with the other kids, some of whom were neighbors, others that lived in town. The Drummer was an excuse for everyone to come out and enjoy the day.

We would return home, the evening sun low, our feet padding softly in the dust. I remember that when I would go with Momma she would explain the news to me and tell me that taxes were necessary and that a citizen must respect the wishes of the government. Momma believed that laws must be obeyed. So, when I would take Goldie and Joli I would give them the same explanation. On our way home we skipped and sang and laughed. We stopped to pick apples from Mr. and Mrs. Cohen's orchard, knowing they wouldn't mind. Life was sweet.

As we came over the hill our home came into sight.

"Race you!" Goldie yelled out.

We all took off running towards our house and the attached flourmill. The overwhelming structure was built by a Russian Czar a century ago. The stone walls were a meter thick and the windowpanes were made of steel to protect the onetime ruler. The rear door of the mill was street level so the farmers could unload their goods. The front of the house had eight steps lead up to the door of the house. While it was more functional than warm and cozy, it was our home. It more than did its job as a place to take care of us both financially, physically, and emotionally.

Upon entering the house, I helped Momma with supper. Joli would always be my assistant. I would always take the job of putting the wood in the stove so Joli wouldn't burn herself. We would then divvy up the remainder of the jobs of stirring the pots, cutting the vegetables, cleaning and doing whatever else we were asked.

Our kitchen was quite large given the time. Besides the oven, stove and sink there was a large wooden table that sat twelve and two couches where my three older brothers slept at night.

Momma was Hungarian and until she had married my Papa she had only spoken Hungarian. She learned Yiddish from my Grandma and Ukrainian from the farmers who came to the mill. We never knew what language would fly of her mouth. Typically, it was Yiddish, the universal language in our home. However, when she was angry or spoke quickly it would always be Hungarian. I had learned all of the languages spoken in the home, just to keep up with what Momma.

Papa owned a lumber depot and Labji and Moshe would work for him after school. After dark, Papa and Labji, the third eldest boy, would come home from the forest or lumber depot and immediately wash up. Papa and my brothers would all gather in the living room and discuss the day, and the ramblings about town. I didn't like being in the kitchen when Papa and my brothers arrived home from their work in the forest or from the city; I wanted to be where I could hear about their world so I always made sure my work in the kitchen was complete by the time they arrived home.

Morci, my other brother, went to college and apprenticed in a large hardware store. He always kissed Momma as soon as he walked through the door; he was her first-born and I had a sneaky suspicion he was her favorite. He was going to go off to the army soon, and we all knew Momma would be sad. We could see the pain in her eyes every time she looked at him.

Moshe had long legs and was a head taller than Morci. His big blue eyes and dark head of hair had made him quite the ladies' man – for this he became the butt of all of our jokes.

Lajbi and I went to school together. His pitch-black hair was in stark contrast to Joli's and my blonde hair. When he wasn't at school or working with Papa in the woods he made sleds and wagons to earn money; he could fix anything.

"How's my little family?" Papa asked, peeking around the corner and smiling. "Ah, Goldie, you're baking bread now?"

Goldie leapt up from the wooden floor, where she had been playing with a wooden mixing bowl and spoon. Papa's curly chestnut brown hair and freckled face matched that of little Goldie's.

"Where are my babies?" he called, searching for the three youngest children.

Pearl, a toe head two-year-old with saucer size blue eyes. would giggle from her hiding place behind the floral couch. Papa would tiptoe into the room, scoop her up and toss and catch her while she screamed with joy. Then it was Goldie's turn to be tossed about and then finally Mendel, a sandy haired 4-year-old, had his turn. Papa would lastly coochi-coo Yidel, who was just a new born.

Papa waved his hands, "enough, enough," as he sat down to catches his breath. Papa leaned back on the sofa and puffed his cigarette.

"Moshe talked to a girl at the Café Star, Momma," Morci shouted.

The Café Star was in the city. It was the place that all the teenagers hung out. I had only been there a few times when I was with the older boys. Momma would tell me that nice girls didn't spend their time at the Café flirting with boys. Nice girls stayed home and helped their family.

"I did not," Moshe said.

"Was that a horse I saw you talking to?" Morci interjected.

We all laughed. Moshe turned red.

"A mare with quite a figure," Papa added.

The boys all burst out laughing.

"I heard that," Momma said.

"Just talking horses," Papa replied, and smiled.

"What's the news?" Papa asked.

That was my cue, the time that Momma would let me leave the kitchen to tell him what I had heard in town. I hustled quickly to the large living room and stood tall in front of him. He glanced at me from beneath his heavy eyebrows. When he smiled his blond mustache would bounce about like a giant caterpillar. His blue eyes would smile too; only when one of us misbehaved did he ever appear stern. He was a very handsome man, of only 40 years.

I told him the daily news: when the gypsies were passing through, and what predator animals were killing the livestock, what ordinances were being discussed. He would discuss what was what in depth and when he finished he would gather us around him and tell us stories of the early days in Vlachovice: how he rebuilt the waterwheel or how he learned to ground the grain into flour. He would tell us family stories: how he met Momma and how he got into the lumber business.

Momma had told me that she was sure Papa was for her when they were first introduced by the matchmaker. My Momma was quite the catch because her dowry was so vast; Papa received a hundred thousand korunas. My Grandpa was Baron Paul Grosman. Grandpa Grosman was a successful businessman who had owned a lucrative business, a large horse farm and even a substantial vineyard that produced wine prior to his death. Papa had a reputation as a playboy. Momma was warned about him, but she knew she wanted him. She had fallen in love instantly.

Everyone in our family always went to bed early so we could rise at first light. Papa and Momma slept in separate beds in the oversized living room. Pearl slept in Momma's bed and Mendel slept in Papa's bed. Goldie slept on the red velvet couch in the living room; Yidel in the crib next to Momma's bed. Joli, Grandma and I slept in one room. I would either sleep in the same bed with Joli or with Grandma on the days she needed me to warm her bed or rub her back. The three older boys slept on the couches in the kitchen. We had a happy life.

The beginning of the end our blissfulness came in 1938 when the Drummer announced that the Germans had asked for the voluntary surrender of the Sudetenland, the western part of

Czechoslovakia. I remember the night I told the news to my Papa. It caused a heated discussion between my family - something that rarely happened.

***

"No one wants a war," Grandma said.

"Who's talking about war?" Momma asked.

"The Germans," Moshe said, "are taking the Sudetenland."

"Let them have it," Momma said. "It's not worth fighting over. Anyway, what's the difference between one government and another? You still have to pay taxes, right?"

"Always taxes," Grandma said, "they'd tax the dead."

We all laughed nervously.

Later that night I laid in bed with Grandma rubbing her back trying to ease her pain. Her thick, loose skin would tumble over my hands as I rolled them over her back and shoulders. Even after all the years of back rubs, I would still cringe as her excess skin and wrinkles covered by tiny fingers. As I ran my hands over the lax skin I could hear my parents talking from the next room. I waited until my grandma slept peacefully to sneak out of bed and down the short hallway. I sat in the corner and pulled my nightdress over my knees and listened hard.

"We should have left long ago to America, when we had the money and papers," Papa said to Momma.

"No," she said. "We are better off here. This is our home. What would've happened to your Mother?"

It wasn't until that night that I knew we had the opportunity to go to America. I had wanted to go to America ever since Papa's sister Sylvia had come to visit us from New York City. She looked so beautiful and fancy dressed in her American clothes – so much younger and more put together than my Momma. I had decided then that I would eventually get to America, "The land of opportunity," as Aunt Sylvia called it as she coaxed my Papa to move us there. My Grandma had threatened to kill herself if we immigrated, so Papa had relented. He had always done whatever it took to please his Mother. He was nothing like his rebellious sister Sylvia. He'd invested his savings in a water wheel instead.

"The war will come here," he said. "The Germans are determined to take the world. Right now they are jailing and persecuting Jews in Germany. They don't want Jews," Papa told her.

Momma sighed and shook her head. Everyone in our family knew that meant she was done listening to that nonsense. My Papa sweetly put his hands on her shoulders and pulled her in for a hug. I snuck away, back to bed. I went to sleep believing that a person as wonderful as my Momma would never be put in jail.

For weeks, our history class discussed the issues going on over the Sudetenland. Each one of the students wanted the teacher to assure them that our treaty partners would not let Czechoslovakia down if the Germans demanded more territory.

In March 1938, the Anschluss, the forced political union of Austria with Germany occurred. Our family sat around our radio to listen to the propaganda of how happy the Austrians were. The announcer on the radio stated that the Austrians were greeting the German army with cheers, flowers and swastika flags.

"How could the Austrian people be happy and cheer, Papa?" I asked.

"My child, many Austrians support the Germans. Even so, Germany is most likely controlling the news," Papa answered, unsure of what to say to us.

"If Germany occupied all of Czechoslovakia many people would cheer," Morci added.

"Morci, what is the purpose of saying such nonsense? That will never happen," Momma spat out.

"Rose," Papa said, "I hear the Gestapo are jailing and hanging Jews. They are stabbed in the streets, their woman raped, their properties set on fire, even while their friends watch."

"Who says such things?" Momma asked.

"The Jews who fled," Papa said.

Momma was still not convinced that all the rumors and stories were true. Or, maybe she just did not want to believe them.

The terrible reports were real to me. As the time passed, I feared Hitler more and more, and I was frightened each time I heard Moshe and Papa relate more reports. Momma ordered there be no more talk of Hitler in the home. I prayed each night that Momma's apparent optimism was well founded.

One year earlier in 1937, Czechoslovakia was in mourning over the death of its first president, Tomas Masaryk. I remember when the teacher announced that Masaryk had died. We all cried. We feared that his successor would hand over the Sudetenland as a gift to Hitler to keep the peace. Under President Benes, our fears came true and the country was never the same. We missed our peaceful lives. Anti-Semitism surfaced and spread like a viral disease eating up the land, first attacking those with low resistance then undermining the rest of the country. Many of our gentile neighbors, whom we had called friends, turned on us, becoming our enemies. Classmates that we had once called friends became our tormentors, "You dirty Jews! What school will you attend when Hitler occupies our country? You will be shipped to Palestine where you belong." A rain of spit, garbage and stones would come down on us. At times it would get so scary. Kids would pull out pocketknives and threaten to cut us when we would walk home from school. There were a few minor injuries to several of the Jewish students before the police would come to our rescue.

Momma would be hysterical while Papa listened intently, and Morci fumed with anger as Lajbi and I took turns explaining what happened each day at school.

"This is a police matter," Momma pleaded, "I am sure they will protect you from now on."

"They attacked us. I would love to give them a bloody nose. One of them called me a dirty Jew bastard," Lajbi protested.

"Please, Samuel, speak to the children. They must learn to live with our neighbors," Momma would plead.

"Momma, you can't blame the boys. Do you expect them to be attacked without defending themselves?" I would argue.

"I know how you feel children. Many times I would have liked to punch some of them myself, but you are no match for those vicious boys or their knives. We are lucky that the police are still on our side," Papa said.

"Rifchu, you must not walk alone to school or home," Papa demanded.

"How can Lajbi be my bodyguard if you say we cannot fight back?" I asked.

"We have knives too, Papa," Lajbi exclaimed, puffing up his chest in frustration.

"Lajbi. Stop! I know you have knives. Momma is right. You must not fight those boys, it will only make matters worse," Papa said.

Momma came in with a cup of tea, "We must live our faith. The Germans will be stopped. I know how you feel when they shear the sheep; the little lambs shiver with fear. But, remember we have strong shepherds in neighboring countries. We must try to ignore the taunts and learn to live with our neighbors until this blows over."

The Drummer still came to our town. I heard the beating of his drum, but the excitement was gone. By late 1938, I didn't care to hear the news he brought.

CHAPTER TWO

UNDER THE HUNGARIANS

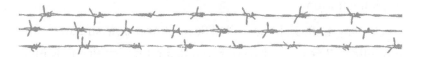

A S PAPA PREDICTED, GERMANY AND Hungary started to dismember Czechoslovakia. In 1938, France, Britain and Italy sanctioned the union of the Sudetenland with Germany in the infamous Munich Pact. Hungary acquired part of Slovakia and the greater part Sub-Carpathia. Bohemia and Moravia became German protectorates and by March 15, 1939, were wholly occupied by German troops. With that, our brave little republic was finished.

The fall of Czechoslovakia ended the political system erected by the Treaty of Versailles at the end of World War I and established Germany as the dominant power in Europe. The Hungarian and German occupation of Czechoslovakia was gradually marked by ruthless exploitation of Czechoslovakian resources and a brutal oppression of its people.

Politics is sometimes distant, meaning that there is no real perceptible effect on the everyday lives of the citizens. This was not the case with the politics of Nazi government. Their political beliefs had a very profound effect on the lives of everyone within their influence. Every resident of Sub-Carpathia fell victim under its new Hungarian masters; but no class of people was to suffer as much as the Jews.

Now that our region was part of Hungary, the population was subject to existing Hungarian laws; for Jews this meant that we would be subject to the anti-Jewish laws already in effect in Hungary; such measures were being taken to quickly deploy implementation.

On May 4, 1939, the so-called Second Anti-Jewish Laws went into effect. These laws were promulgated under Prime Minister Count Paul Teleki. He was not a full-blown Nazi but was a champion of a brand of anti-Semitism that may be described as "civilized;" that is, he was not a rabid street dog on the subject of Jews. He was especially kinder to the so-called native "Magyarized" Jews, who were culturally assimilated into Hungarian life. Teleki, however, became a vitriolic anti-Semite on the matter of what he called the "Eastern Jews," the Jews who lived in the newly absorbed territories. Teleki resented the distinctiveness of these "foreign Jews," many of whom were Orthodox, whose lifestyle, dress customs and ethical codes were alien to him. Furthermore, he, like other anti-Semites, thought the Jews were dangerous because of their influential role in Hungary's economic and cultural life. These views, of course, coincided with the official attitudes towards Jews in Germany, Austria and the territories they absorbed after the Anschluss.

The provisions of the Second Anti-Jewish Laws were wide-sweeping and aimed at restricting the participation of Jews in public and economic life. The laws prohibited Jews from obtaining Hungarian citizenship, holding government positions and greatly restricted civil rights. It forced the resignation of

Jewish members of the court. It dismissed all Jewish primary and secondary school teachers. Very few Jews were exempt from the new laws; decorated war heroes, university professors and Olympic champions were some of the very few to escape the initial persecution.

The economic opportunities for Jews became severely limited. A quota system was put in place for the number of Jews allowed to own businesses. The purpose of this law was to limit Jews in leadership positions and from participating actively and freely in the economic life of the country.

Instead of appeasing the anti-Semites in Hungary, as many moderates thought it would, the law only increased anti-Semitism. Two years later, a Third Anti-Jewish Law was put in order. This law exhibited even greater anti-Semitism; it defined Jews as members of a new racial group. This latest law prohibited marriage or extramarital relations between Jews and non-Jews. The law further narrowed the definition of "who is a Jew," even classifying Jewish converts to Christianity as being Jews first and forever.

Each month the anti-Semitic measures brought new forms of prejudice. Non-Jewish students were automatically accepted in the esteemed schools, but Jewish students could enroll only after passing extremely difficult examinations. The rigorous tests were created so that only a small percentage of Jewish students managed to overcome the barrier to enter into schools.

Prior to this law, I had been enrolled in a private school that closed during all the turmoil. Lajbi, Joli and I were allowed to sit for the exam to the new school systems. Lajbi and I both passed the exams, Joli didn't. We were to start attending the new Hungarian public school system. As time went on most of the Jewish families didn't feel that an education was worth the harassment or the risk. My Momma was not on the same page as those parents. She felt that an education was the most valuable thing anyone could ever have. *If you had your brain and your wits you could solve any problem.* I loved learning and took advantage of my opportunity to get an education. I studied hard and in a matter of year I was in the same grade as Lajbi. I learned to speak and read Russian and German; this was on top of the Hungarian, Yiddish and Ukrainian that I already spoke.

In addition to encouraging me to go to school and learn, my Momma taught me skills that she felt would make up for my small stature. She taught me to sew and got me even more involved with the tasks in the mill. She told me to think and use my brain; that my intelligence would be my greatest strength.

For the first time money had become scarce and I had to earn extra money for my school supplies. I began doing homework for other kids in my class. I would secretly slip them their paper before class and they would hand me the money and go on their way; pretending that they weren't fraternizing with a Jew.

★★★

The government eventually put a new law into place to restrict how much grain a farmer could have in their possession at any one time. It had become the job of the mills to help the Nazis monitor and ration out the farmer's grain. Each week soldiers would come to our mill and take anything over the allotted amount that the farmers and the mills were authorized to have in their possession. The amount that the government ruled that the farmers and we were allowed to keep would not have been enough to feed our family, let alone sell.

My Momma had taught me how to work the mill including weighing and measuring the grain and flour. My Momma had decided that we would "cheat" the Nazis by cheating the scale. She knew that the Nazis may expect an adult to cheat them, but they would never expect a child to be brave enough to defy them so she taught me how to manipulate the scale.

"Always look them in the eyes," Momma said, "that way if your eyes and their eyes are locked, they won't be looking at what your hands and feet are doing."

There was a large table set up in the mill. Next to the table was a large cast iron castor wheel grain scale. When the soldiers came to gather the grain Momma would stand off to the side. I would stand bravely in front of the officers. I had a book with the amount of grain each of the farmers had brought to us to mill. I was given my orders of how much each farmer was rationed and what was to be given to the government. I would carefully add the grain to the pan that hung from the iron arms, I would then slip my foot gently under the base of the scale, never taking my eyes off of the soldiers. I was able to manipulate the scale with my foot, saving several kilograms for both the farmers and us. I would then wrap the grain up for them, look them in the eyes, trying to burn them and sweetly say, "Have a nice day."

After every encounter my Momma would say the same thing as if she had recorded it, "You did so good, my big brave girl. Let's not tell Papa."

We all tried to adjust to the new regime but it was difficult to overlook the severe and growing suppression of Jews and our status as second-class citizens. Momma, as was her habit, tried to spin it and put the best light on things. She frequently tried to make us look at the happier side of our condition, although not much happiness remained under the new order.

"They are not such bad people," Momma would say, referring to the new government officials.

I think she really did see the good in them at times, or at least she tried to. She would excuse some of their behavior by saying they were misguided and momentarily being influenced by the professional Jew-haters. Some may have said Momma was being naïve but I believe she needed this to keep her sanity. For her, it was easier to sweep things under the rug than to look at the big mess piled up right in front of her face.

If she was being naïve it wasn't apparent to me at the time. I was deeply influenced by my Momma's attitudes toward things. My Momma was my world. She brought me hope. However, it was hard for that hope to last very long. We were gradually becoming victims of the worsening situation and it was obvious that it would soon become life threatening.

Admiral Miklos Horthy was the Regent of the Kingdom of Hungary from March 1, 1920 until October 15, 1944. His admiral's title may have seemed odd for a country that is landlocked, but Horthy got his title under the former Austro-Hungarian Empire, a vast territorial expanse that included lands on the Adriatic Sea on which the empire had a naval force. Horthy had a long history of anti-communism and he was vigilant in ferreting out leftward-leaning movements. His policies were certainly not antagonistic to the new programs of German Nazis. Yet he was Hungarian first and foremost. He looked upon German expansion with both favor and fear. Try as he did to maintain the independence of Hungary, he had to walk a tight rope of diplomacy to avoid antagonizing the German Reich. Horthy personally had little use for the Jews, and to appease the Nazis and the anti-Semitic factions in his government, he appointed certain rabid anti-Semites to official positions. Propaganda against the Jews, always a minority in Eastern Europe, came out into the open and had the full backing and support of the government.

Hitler's book *Mein Kampf* became mandatory school reading as well as a best seller in stores. One day Morci came home from college with a copy of *Mein Kampf* and another anti-Semitic book authored by a Hungarian who claimed to be an authority on racial genetics. Like Hitler's book, the tone on racial genetics held that Jews were genetic carriers of degenerative diseases. Jews by virtue of their many centuries of imposed seclusion were according to the racist theorist, "a distinct biological race." With such theories being in vogue in Germany and Hungary what was soon to happen in the death camps was inevitable.

***

In late August 1939, the Drummer gave us the tragic news that Stalin had signed a nonaggression pact with Hitler. What the Drummer did not announce that month was that the two dictators agreed to carve up Poland. The Germans moved first. They invaded Poland the following month. The Poles tried resisting. The British came to the aid of the Poles and declared war on Germany, thus World War II began.

At thirteen years old, all of these events were too difficult for me to fully comprehend. I did know that my parents truly believed that France, Great Britain, and the other European democracies would not permit things to degenerate more than they already had. We were all convinced that the Allies would soon crush Hitler. We had prepared ourselves for continued suffering, even increased suffering, but no one believed that the war would take the turn it did. With the rest of the world against Hitler we never thought that he would so easily hold Europe in his iron fist.

It was not long before the government ordered the deportation of Polish Jews residing in Sub-Carpathia and elsewhere in the newly acquired lands in Hungary. All Jews whose Fathers, Mothers, or Grandparents were of Polish origin were to report to a government center for transfer to Poland. The government explained that the Poles were needed to work in the fields in their ancestral land. Polish gentiles were exempt from deportation. The deportation, of course, served its intended purposes: the Germans got their hands on the Jews and the Hungarians rid themselves of the unwanted Polish Jews.

The deportation order of the Polish Jews scared everyone. We all were going to be losing family and friends. Our family was very close with a Polish family who lived near our town. Their oldest son, Morre, was Moshe's best friend; the two went to high school together.

Morre's Father had come from Poland before Morre was born. He was a hard working shoemaker and ran one of the most popular shoe shops in town. Two days after the deportation decree, Papa went to see Morre's Father; Papa knew of the decree but he felt it would not affect Morre's family for weeks, at least enough time for him to sell his shoe business and house, to get a team of horses and to pack belongings.

Papa returned from Morre's house near sunset.

"Samuel how is Morre's family? How are they handling news of the order?" Momma asked.

"They are gone, Rose," Papa said.

"How can they be gone? It has been but two days."

"Others live in the house already," Papa said a confusion in his voice that I had never heard before.

"Others?" Momma couldn't believe what she was hearing.

"The neighbor said that Gendarmes came during the night and forced them to leave," Papa said.

"But Samuel, how could they leave without selling their house?"

"The police made them leave."

"But how can that be true? What sort of government would make a man move out of his house without giving him time to sell it?"

"Our government, Rose," Papa replied.

"And who lives there now?" Momma said, confused.

"Hungarian collaborators."

"I don't believe that," Momma said.

He shrugged, "I'm just telling you what I saw and what I was told."

"I don't believe this. It's impossible," Momma said over and over again. "Did you stop on your way to visit with your sister?" She asked changing the subject.

"Yes, I did and found her very upset. She had received a letter from her son in Bratislava. Simon wrote that he is troubled about the increase of anti-Semitism in Slovakia. It isn't easy being a Rabbi. It isn't easy to lead a worried congregation."

"It is a shame. That man struggled to become a rabbi and now this. It will simmer down," Momma said, an unrealistic hope in her voice.

I was listening from my room, my ear pressed to the door to hear what my parents were saying. What Papa described didn't surprise me. I had seen what was occurring even in our town: the insulting torments for being a Jew; the many times we were mocked and pushed around.

We all felt the new mood in town. One day, one of Momma's best customers at the mill exploded at her in anger.

"You're prices of grain are much too high," the customer yelled, "I can get my grain milled somewhere else for half of the price!"

"Sir, please, I apologize. My prices haven't changed for years. I am sorry you feel that way," Momma said sweetly.

The customer shouted back, "You see, it's been going on for years and I didn't even know it. You Jews..." He stalked off and never returned.

Papa was also having similar troubles in his lumber delivery business.

Suspicion and persecution of Jews continued to spread. One day, Morci came into the house looking very agitated. "They just took over the factories and mills in Poland," he said. "I've heard they are throwing Jews out of their homes and businesses in Poland. If you want a Jew's clothes, you just walk up to him in the street, hit him over the head with a club and take them. It's that simple."

For the moment it was that simple. But what we didn't realize was how lucky we were at the time.

CHAPTER THREE

THE KNOCK AT THE DOOR

I T DIDN'T TAKE LONG FOR Hungary to deport all of the Polish Jews. And they didn't stop there. Once they finished with the Poles, Hungary issued a new decree: Jews who failed to prove Hungarian citizenship were to be transported to Ukraine, and later to Poland. The government defined Hungary by its original boundaries that didn't include the land taken from Czechoslovakia. Only Momma could prove Hungarian citizenship. The rest of the family was considered Czechs and subject to deportation.

"They can't just move us. We have friends in the government. You must talk to them Samuel," Momma pleaded.

Papa did "talk to them." He bribed a long-time family friend, a government official, giving him part of our farmland and promising to deliver him flour every week in exchange for our legal designation as Hungarian Jews. He happily took the land and goods. The official, with whom my Papa at was at one time such a good friend, condescendingly told him, "I've been offered twice as much by other Jews. I do it for you because of friend-ship."

"Friendship! Why, they are no better than the Nazis," Momma yelled as Papa told her the story.

"Momma, please try to understand, it's very dangerous to help Jews," Morci told her.

"Since when do you pay friends for helping you? Did I ask him for money when I nursed his wife back to health? Did you ask him for money when you gave him a horse for plowing?" Momma sputtered in frustration.

When I went to bed that night, Momma was still pacing around the living room ranting to herself about all she had done for that 'friend.'

***

It was bitterly cold night. The thick wet snowflakes caked the windows. The wind moaned and howled with each forceful gust. I couldn't be sure when I heard the banging if it was a knock on the door or the wrapping of a branch on the roof. But then I heard it again, we all did. My brothers swarmed to the living room, as did I, as we waited for my Papa to make his way to the kitchen door. The ice and frost caked glass made it impossible to see who was at the door.

"Stay here," Papa said.

We did as we were told. My heart was pounding. Was it our time to be taken from our home? My brothers and I peeked around the wall as Papa opened the door. I held my breath as he slowly twisted the knob. A fierce white flurry blew through the kitchen and carpeted the floor.

"Morre," I heard Papa say. "Morre...what are you doing boy, what are you doing out in such weather? Come in and sit by the fire."

Momma ran into the kitchen, "Who would let a boy out like this? Where is your coat? Where are your boots?"

I exhaled. It was Moshe's best friend.

"I...I....I came..." I couldn't understand what Morre was through his chattering teeth.

"Rose, heat up some soup."

Morre had walked to our house from Poland, several hundred kilometers from Vlachovice. He didn't have on a hat, gloves or shoes; only had rags wrapped around his face, hands and feet.

"There was no place else to go," he said. "All is lost. Everywhere...everything is lost." Morre warmed himself on the bowl of soap as he ate. Tears fell from his eyes while he told his story. He said that his Papa and Momma were dead. Morre and his family were marched to the center of town where thousands of people were gathered at gunpoint.

The commotion had woken up the rest of the family. Now, everyone was in the kitchen. We all sat around Morre, hanging on his every word.

"And the others?" Papa asked.

"Dead," Morre said. "Every Jew that left Hungary with us is dead."

"I don't believe it," Momma said. "They wouldn't kill that many people; there were thousands of deportees."

"It's not easy to imagine it. But I saw it. I saw people left in the forest without food. I saw Jews packed in synagogues that were then set on fire. I saw Jews lined up and executed," he grimaced bitterly at his own descriptions.

He went on with his horrifying reporting. He told of Jews being tied to windmills and used for target practice, of Jews being crammed into cattle-car trains and taken deeper into Poland to camps where they were murdered - camps with names like Treblinka. Death camps - that is what he called them.

"Two nights ago I saw a Momma smother her own child to death to save us from being found by the SS."

"How can a Momma kill her own child?" Momma cried.

"She did not mean to kill the child. The guy smuggling us across the border ordered her to stuff a scarf into the child's mouth to stop it from crying. We could all have been shot if we were discovered. Killing Jews is a profitable business. They take our money to betray or kill us. I could not make up such stories. I saw my Papa shot through the head by a Hungarian policeman on our way to Poland. Papa had asked where he could find water for his horse and the Hungarian policeman shot him. He laughed saying 'I did you a favor, Jews. You'll thank me later.' And when my Momma screamed 'You beast,' he shot her too. He didn't bat an eye. And there are thousands of men like that policeman. Believe me; your neighbors may shoot you. We are all fugitives. We don't have a place to go. We will all be dead soon. Nothing can save us. Nothing."

Papa, Moshe, Morci, and Lajbi listened to Morre through the night. Momma kept quiet. Momma sent the rest of the kids to bed. I finally decided I couldn't take anymore and I also went back to bed with Grandma. I slipped into bed and snuggled next to her. I hugged her and rubbed her back until she fell back to sleep.

I lay awake in the darkness. I couldn't hear what was being said in the kitchen, nor did I want to. All I knew was that a terror had washed over our house and things would never be the same.

We hid Morre in the hayloft of our stables for over a week. It wasn't safe enough for either him or us to let him stay in the house. Momma gave him a winter coat, boots and some money. Morre headed out for his old home to find his Mother's diamond ring that his Father had hidden in the backyard. He wanted to use it to buy Hungarian citizenship papers or "gentile papers" and a ticket to Budapest, where no one could identify him. A week later, on a starless night, Morre said his goodbyes and set off on foot. We never heard from him again.

CHAPTER FOUR

SPRING IN MUKACHEVE

MY FAVORITE SEASON WAS ALWAYS SPRING, the snow recedes away from the hills and the lush green grass emerges, the trees begin to bud, the fields take color and the flowers bloom. I always felt that if the world could survive the winter then anything was possible. The spring of 1943 was my final semester before graduation, and I was filled with anticipation, the sun brought hope, even amid the bad news that we heard every day.

In June, I walked to the podium to accept my high school diploma and bid goodbye to my teachers, as was custom. For two years, I was the only Jewish student in the class. Lajbi had dropped out after a year. I was left alone to take the abuse and bullying of the students. I had been glued to my chair, chased down, threatened, but I had stood tall. I had even withstood the mockery by my teacher.

On the first day I had attended this school I had received a lecture and a warning from my teacher, "I see you decided to join our school. We shall see what you learned in your school. We shall see how long you will be able to keep up with my class."

She stood in front of the first row, facing me with her arms folded and a fake smile on her bulldog face. The thirty gentile students responded to her taunting with an uproar of laughter, while I stood silent, helplessly burning from humiliation and anger.

I was not only proud that I had made it through school but also relieved. I was tormented each day I was in class but I was determined to graduate. Nothing was going to get in my way. So there I was, in front of my tormentors – accepting my diploma – all I could do was smile.

I always knew it was the first day of summer when Grandma pulled out her Tachrichim, the traditional white linen death shroud that she had my Momma make her when I was ten-years-old. Grandma had been planning on dying for six years now. Each year she didn't die she was worried that her Tachrichim wasn't white enough so she would bleach it, wash it, dry it and try it on to make sure it still fit.

Grandma and I had a special relationship so I was the one she would choose to try on her burial outfit for each year.

"Rifchu, how do I look?" Grandma asked, "This is what I am going to wear when I die. I want to look good."

She did this every single year. She was always very pleased with herself that it still fit. No matter how old a woman gets vanity never ceases to escape them.

"You look good, Grandma," I said, rather uncomfortable that I was looking at what my Grandma was going to look like when she was dead. She would smile and take the shroud off and neatly pack it back into a box and wait until next summer when she would do it all again.

The rest of my summer, I enjoyed helping Momma in the garden, canning fruits and vegetables and working in the mill.

***

The Drummer's news grew ever gloomier for the town's Jews. Jews were no longer allowed to attend school, even religious schools. Jews needed permits to leave town. Jews needed permits to work. We were made to wear armbands adorned with a Jewish star on it so others would be able to easily distinguish that we were Jews. We had become prisoners of our own communities.

By autumn I was desperate to get out of our small village. Papa agreed to help me. He paid for a work permit for me to be a dressmaker in Mukacheve. I was to learn to sew and design fine garments. I was excited about my new opportunity and overall anxious to get out of the house and see the city. I took the train to and from work with my brothers and Papa.

My first few days in the city were exciting. Although I felt like a bird released from captivity, I was, in fact, in danger. Hungarian police and the Gestapo were everywhere. The restrictions for Jews were numerous. Cinemas and city property and parks were off limits. Signs on stores read: WE DON'T SERVE JEWS. JEWS ARE NOT WELCOME HERE. NO TRESSPASSING FOR JEWS OR DOGS.

Even sympatric merchants posted these signs; open sympathy for Jews was a crime. At night Jewish youths destroyed many of the signs risking harsh punishments if caught.

One Sunday I ran into one of my neighbors, Mr. Vasel, in the city. He had lived in the farm next to ours since I was little girl. Before the anti-Jewish movement his son and I had been friends. As our closest neighbors, the Vasel boys would play with my siblings and I all the time but when anti-Semitism set in, that quickly changed.

Mr. Vasel approached me. He motioned to my armband, "You could be free of this. You can become Catholic and marry my son. You will be the daughter I always wanted. Why suffer, when you don't even look Jewish?" he asked, referring to my blonde hair and ice blue eyes.

I knew he was being kind but I had no intention of turning my back on my faith or my family. And even more so, I was a romantic and was going to marry for love. "Mr. Vasel, I like being Jewish and I have parents. Even if he was Jewish, I wouldn't want to marry your son just to escape persecution, that isn't right for me or your son. All this will change when the war is over."

"I respect your decision, Rifcha, but it is not a smart one," Mr. Vasel said to me politely.

Mr. Vasel was probably right but I would not compromise my values. Plus, I was enjoying the thrills and delights of city life, the biggest delight being Jacob, my first boyfriend. We had met on the train to work. He lived in a small village near mine. After work Jacob and I would meet in the ice-cream parlor. I was sixteen and in love for the first time. He made my heart flutter, sing and soar. Being with Jacob made the world around me seem to disappear. Jacob did his best to make the cruelties around us fade away.

One day while on an afternoon walk through the heart of the city I said to Jacob, "I wish we could go see a movie." I don't know why I said it. I really didn't even want to go to the movie. I just wanted to be able to go.

"Let's go then!" he said, always wanting to see me smile.

"Jacob, it's forbidden," I whispered to him.

"Follow me," he said leading me towards an alleyway.

Once tucked away in the shadows, Jacob took off the yellow stars that were pinned to our chests. I tried to pull the shabby marking back into my body but Jacob was tugged it away and stuffed it into his pants pocket.

"We can get in so much trouble for this," I said.

"Only if we get caught," he said with a grin.

Jacob took my hand and walked us out of the darkness and towards the movie theatre. Just like in the flourmill I stood up straight and pretended nothing scared me but I was terrified. We purposely arrived at the cinema late, taking our seats just as the pre-roll footage was starting to play.

The world news flashed across the screen: The image of Hitler barking orders to his followers, his voice seethed with hatred. The German youth marched like toy soldiers hailing the devil. Hitler's thousands of followers shouted "Sieg Heil." I suddenly felt ill. My palms became sweaty and my stomach began to churn. I tried not to jump from my seat and run. I was sure they were going to march off the screen and trample me. I was terrified by the show of evil force and the immense impact Hitler was having on everyone around us. I sat quivering in fear as the movie began.

The feature film was a love story, but I could not relax enough to enjoy it. Jacob took my hand and intertwined his fingers in mine. I tried desperately to live in the moment but I couldn't. I was filled with foreboding the image of the Nazi fingers pointing at me from every direction: You are a Jew without your yellow star on your chest!

Jacob's warm breath and soft words filled my ears, "Don't look so sad. We can be happy if you love me as much as I love you." He kissed my forehead. His lips felt warm on my face. But I wasn't able to go to our safe place, the special place where love was the only thing that mattered. We walked out of the theater in silence. The sidewalk was crowded with people free from the star. The fall air chilled my body and I began to shiver. We turned down the first alley. In the shadows, Jacob pinned my yellow star back on my shirt with pride and care as if it was a beautiful corsage, but I looked away as if he was branding me: the hated one.

"We will have a happy future, Rifka. You will see. Happy and married with lots of babies," Jacob said a big grin across his face.

"How can you think of happiness for us when our future is so uncertain? How can you think of commitments when you are drafted to serve in the Hungarian labor force? Even the Jewish men who were once soldiers had their guns replaced with shovels. You will be shipped out to the Russian front to dig trenches for the Germans. If that doesn't kill you, the Nazis will," I sputtered at him everything that came to my mind.

"I will come back, you must believe that," Jacob said.

"Do you really believe that? Has anyone returned yet?"

"The Germans are in retreat. The war will be over soon, and until then we have to hold on. Have some faith," he told me.

CHAPTER FIVE

PASSOVER

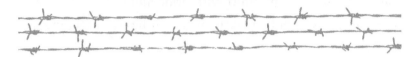

I N FEBRUARY OF 1944, a month before Passover, Grandma suddenly got sick and died peacefully in her sleep. We had a small funeral service for her at the house. She was dressed in her Tachrichim that she had washed, bleached and tried on the previous summer. Grandma was buried in a Jewish cemetery. Her final resting place was next to my sister Hannah who had died when I was four-years-old. Hannah died while my Momma was pregnant with Goldie. She had died of pneumonia. I had rocked her to sleep the night before she died and for months was convinced that it was my fault that she died. To help me get over the guilt of Hannah, when Goldie was born, Momma put her in my arms and said, "Here is your baby."

Goldie clung to me at Grandma's funeral, "Grandma is in a better place," I whispered to her.

Papa searched the graveyard for a large stone. When he finally found one he placed it on the head of Grandma's burial plot. "So, we will always be able to find her," Papa said.

In the Jewish religion it is tradition to wait a year to place a headstone on a gravesite. But Papa must have known we weren't going to be here in year.

***

As the deportations continued most of the people in Vlacho-vice stopped speaking to us because we were Jews. The Hungarian police had been infiltrated and overtaken by Hungarian Nazis. These Nazis took special pleasure in molesting and attacking the Jewish girls. "Jew girls sleep with their fathers. At least you can do is sleep with me," was the common insult. The police in nearby towns were raping the girls and there was no one to turn to for help. Times were getting even more desperate.

On Passover, Moses had saved the Jewish nation from Egyptians. He had performed miracle after miracle until the Pharaoh set the Israelites free in the great Exodus. Certainly, we thought, God could perform a miracle and save us from the Nazis. God would surely save the innocent.

That is what we prayed for, even though we heard of Jews being beaten, shot, burned, raped, and enslaved. We couldn't figure out why the Germans wanted to kill Jews. Didn't they have enough to do defending themselves from the British, Russians and Americans?

Momma would say, "The Americans will save us...the war will be over soon; we can count on President Roosevelt, he will come, if not, God will come."

"No one will come," Papa would respond. "President Roosevelt is worried about Hitler and Japan, not the Jews."

With hopeful and desperate prayers and thoughts we prepared to celebrate Passover. As was custom, we repainted the house. We turned the walls blue, Grandma's favorite color. She always said no matter how awful life is, you can always look at the sky and say, "I am grateful for the blue sky." And we were grateful. We were grateful we had a roof over our heads. We were grateful we still had the flourmill and food on the table. We were grateful that we all still had each other.

We finished our spring-cleaning. Our home was spotless. The walls looked like the clear blue sky. All that was left was for Papa to arrive home. We sat on the outside stairs waiting for him to appear on the dirt path. The sun began setting behind the grove of oaks. It wasn't like Papa to be this late. Momma stared down the empty road that led to the town Chynadiyovo.

"You don't think something happened?" I whispered.

"No" Lajbi said too quickly. I could tell he was worried, too.

"Papa can take care of himself," Moshe said sternly.

"Even against the Nyilas?" I asked. The Nylias were Hungarian Nazis, members of the Arrow Cross Party. They wore khaki uniforms and stormed around like their fellow Nazis in Germany. They took pleasure in committing cruelties against Jews and otherwise demonstrating their loyalty to the German Fuhrer.

Momma now stood at the steps shading her eyes from the last rays of sun and looking anxiously toward town. She turned and said, "Let's finish cooking supper." I had never seen her so nervous.

"Just go sit on the steps Momma. Joli and I can finish cooking," I said.

It took some coaxing, but we finally got her to sit down. Joli and I went into the kitchen to cook. I felt like I was in a pressure cooker. I went through each movement of preparing dinner trying to control my breathing, waiting for Papa to appear.

Finally, we heard Momma's familiar "Ah, ha!" which could only mean that Papa and Morci were in sight. "You think because you are the husband of a patient woman you can come home any time you like?" she said with tears in her eyes. They hugged each other tightly. Morci passed by them and came up the stairs.

"The Passover food smells good," Morci said as he hurried past me.

I ran from the stove and chased Morci into the living room, "Come on, Morci, tell me what's wrong," I pleaded.

"We only know that Mukacheve is swarming with Gestapo, SS, and the Hungarian gendarmes. We missed the train because there were so many checkpoints. We were lucky to have hitch-hiked home."

"Could it be because of the Jewish soldiers passing through in the last weeks?"

"I don't know Rifcha. Let's keep this from the little ones. No need to scare everyone."

The last Seder in our house was the saddest one not only for us but also for the other six Jewish men my Papa had invited to join us for the feast. The six men were in the Hungarian labor force and were staying in night Chynadiyovo on their way to the Russian front. Momma's holiday duties kept her cheerful and busy that night. But Papa, my brothers and I were sad. We knew after tonight the men would continue their march and we would likely never see or hear from them again. The war dominated the Passover conversation.

"The German's have been driven back by the Russians," Labji said.

"They've been beaten in Italy, too," Moshe said.

"The war will be over soon," Lajbi said.

"At least if the Germans are losing the war they can't much care about killing the Jews," Moshe added.

"Moshe, I told you there will be no talk of such lies of killing of Jews in this house," Momma said. Moshe started to protest but Momma gazed towards the younger children who sat scared in their seats. Moshe quickly understood and changed the topic.

"Dinner is delicious, Momma."

CHAPTER SIX

HOUSE ARREST

I T WAS A COOL APRIL DAY, the Sunday after Passover. The fog hung low in the valley like the lurking sadness that hung in our hearts. Papa decided that he must know what was going on in the city and no matter how hard Momma protested, Papa insisted. He kissed Momma and wiped away her tears and headed out towards Chynadiyovo. I watched him out the window. He faded quickly into the fog.

Papa knew well enough to keep cover, so he walked along, ducking into the brush when he saw anyone. When he came to the Latorica Bridge he had no choice but to address the Gendarme, and hope he could cross. Papa approached the Gendarme who sat straight back atop his thoroughbred. The Gendarme turned out to be an old family friend. Papa thought that he may be in luck. He and the Gendarme used to play cards together, they had many good laughs back in the day. As Papa approached, the Gendarme whipped his nightstick down at Papa, almost clubbing him on the head.

"Don't you recognize me?" Papa asked.

"Yes, I do Mr. Kalus but I have orders to turn back the Jews."

"Only the Jews?"

"Yes," the Gendarme replied.

"Can you please tell me why?" Papa asked.

"No, Mr. Kalus, I cannot. Now, turn around and go back to where you came from."

Papa tipped his hat to his old friend and headed home.

Momma and I were preparing lunch when Papa returned home. We could tell right away that something was wrong. The room lingered in silence. We waited for Papa to speak. I could feel the room bubbling and I thought I was going to burst if he didn't say something soon.

"I fear the Jews are in trouble on the other side of the bridge. I fear for us, too," was all Papa said before heading into the living room.

I couldn't breathe. I couldn't stand the tension in the house. I thought if I got outside somehow the fear would dissipate. So I ran. There was a spot on top of a hill where I could see across the river to Chynadiyovo. I thought that if I could see something that we would find that Papa was just imagining things, that everything was okay on the other side of the river.

I stood perched atop the hill, from there, I could see the red slate roof of the three-story stone building that we called "the torture chamber." The building housed the Secret Police, Gestapo, Arrow Cross, Gendarmes and political prisoners. The brick wall surrounding the building hid many secrets from the public. But other than the inside those walls, from where I stood, nothing seemed out of the norm on the other side of the bridge.

★ ★ ★

In spite of all the fears surrounding us, my friends and I managed to muster up the ability for some normalcy of teenage life. As the weather began to warm, there were picnics and gatherings to attend. And, I still had Jacob. At least for the moment. That was until the order for house arrest came for the Jews across the river. That was what was what was to put an end to whatever normalcies we had left.

Two days before the order came down Jacob and I had been at a picnic with our friends. He looked so handsome, his sandy brown hair blowing in the breeze and the specs of green in his hazel eyes sparkling in the sun. He had gallantly spread out his jacket on the ground as we sat together with our friends. We all laughed and talked as if our world wasn't coming to an end. We spoke of impossible futures and gossiped as if there wasn't imminent doom awaiting us.

I was busy chatting with one of my girlfriends when Jacob got up and walked to the bank of the river. When I noticed he was gone I excused myself to see if he was all right. He was sitting and staring at the glistening water. I tiptoed over and tapped him on the shoulder. When he turned, I could see that he had been crying. He quickly wiped his tears.

"What's wrong? Why are you crying?" I asked

"Because of you... because I love you... because I know I could lose you."

I knelt down and held him. I had no words to comfort him. He was right.

"I'm leaving with the Hungarian military for Poland. I may never come back or..." his words trailed off.

"Jacob, promise me to take care of yourself and stay alive. Who knows what will happen. I might die if I have to go to Poland or if some of the other rumors we have heard are true.... You know how strong I am," I said as I made a muscle with my very skinny arm. I had hoped it would garner a smile out of him. It didn't. "Just take care of yourself," I said without knowing what else to say. Jacob took my hand and held it. We sat and watched the river in silence, the laughter of our friends murmuring in the background.

★★★

Two days later, when I got the news that the Jews across the river, including Jacob, were under house arrest I knew I had to see him just one more time. I had to tell him I love him, but I knew my parents would never let me try to sneak across to the other side of the river.

I knew what I had to do. I woke up early the next morning while everyone in my house slept. I dressed myself to look like a peasant girl and quietly left the house. I hurried down the path and across the fields, the morning dew dampened the edges of my long black skirt. A tattered scarf hung over my rough white linen blouse. On my arm was a woven basket that carried a few eggs, walnuts and vegetables. I covered it with an old paisley handkerchief. To finish my disguise, I got a crucifix from our mill hand and placed it on top of the handkerchief.

I came to a dead stop at the bridge that crossed over to Chynadiyovo where Jacob lived. My heart pounded. I knew that if I was I caught I could be turned over to the brutal Nyilas. The same Gendarme who stood guard when my Papa came across was there again. He had been to our house before and I knew that he could possibly recognize me. As I approached, I kept my head bowed, "Good morning," I said.

"What is this?" he asked staring at me and pressing his bayonet against my chest.

"Can't a poor gentile girl deliver eggs and feed her family?" I asked.

He uncovered the basket. He pushed the goods around to verify the contents. He seemed satisfied and motioned me to cross the bridge. I first went to the gentile section in case the Gendarme was watching. I then backtracked to Jacob's house.

It was a beautiful day but there weren't any children outside playing. There weren't any people on their way to market or to the local businesses. No one was working outside in their yards or fixing up their homes. The silence was haunting. I could taste the tears in the air.

Jacob lived next to the synagogue. His house appeared to be deserted. I looked around before I knocked on his door. His mother answered, I could tell she had been crying. She threw her arms around me. I felt the weight of her body fall upon my shoulders, and I knew that Jacob wasn't there. She told me that the Gestapo had come at dawn. When her husband had opened the door, a machine gun was shoved into his face and he was ordered into the street to join the other Jews. The Mayor was there with a registration sheet to make sure that every Jewish man was present and accounted for. They took Jacob and the other men to the schoolyard. As far as she knew, the men were being sent to Mukacheve to work.

"If you see him again, please tell Jacob that I love him," I said.

She pressed my hands between hers. "Run, child," she said, "If I see him again I will give him your message. He loves you so. I know it will give him hope." She began to cry again. I hugged her and she pushed me away, "Go on, child, hurry, before the Gestapo return."

I ran home as fast as I could. There was a type of fear and anger that I never felt before was burning in my soul. I burst through the kitchen door and fell to the floor. My ears were ringing and my heart was breaking. Momma began to yell about how frightened she was that I was missing but I couldn't hear her over the sound of my pounding heart.

"You scared me so bad!" Momma yelled.

Thump thump. Thump thump. My head began to overtake my pounding heart.

"Jacob is gone. Gone. Already!" I said, tears flooding over my eyelids.

"Everything is happening faster than I thought," Papa said at the table. "They may come tonight or tomorrow; we must be ready." I saw my Momma's face; she no longer could deny what was happening. I had never seen her so frightened before.

Momma hurried to the kitchen and began baking biscuits, bread, and cookies. My brothers helped Papa prepare the wagon.

As we worked, I told Momma, "Morci, Moshe Lajbi and I could have gone, two months earlier, and joined the Ukraine partisans in the Carpathian forests. I would rather die fighting than to be taken to Mukacheve to be starved and raped by the Nazis."

"You could have been raped and killed there, too. The boys would have faced a firing squad as soon as it was discovered they were Jewish. The partisans don't want Jews. Be patient, the Russians are advancing. We will be together until we are freed."

"Momma, you have been saying that for years, and now it is over for us," I said.

Momma couldn't be disabused of her optimism, "You heard the BBC radio only two days ago. Hitler is losing ground on all fronts. German cities are being heavily bombed. The war can't go on much longer. We will wait and God willing we will all be safe."

The government had ordered all Jews to give up their radios several months ago. The police came around and gathered them up. We complied with the order and turned over our radio. Papa went the next day and purchased another one on the black market. News and knowledge was power. Papa made sure we were never left in the dark.

The next day Papa had gone into the city to find out whatever he could about the worsening situation. We were all nervous but understood that Papa knew what he was doing. I heard his slow heavy tread trek up the steps just before suppertime. He walked into the kitchen.

"Papa," Pearl shouted, running into the kitchen. He turned to pick up Pearl, lifting her higher and higher as she screamed in delight.

"Supper, Papa?" I said.

"It can wait, Rifchu." he said. "I have something to say first."

"Is the war over?" Lajbi asked.

Papa shook his head, "I'm afraid the war is not over."

"But the Germans are being beaten by the Russians," Lajbi said.

The look on Papa's face said it all. Momma tried to stay strong but this was the first time that even she couldn't hold back the tears. Papa cleared his throat, "We must all gather a few of our favorite belongings. We should be prepared to leave as soon as tomorrow morning."

"But Papa, they can't make us leave," Lajbi said.

"They don't have the right," Moshe added. He was about to cry.

"They are the government. We don't have a choice," Papa said firmly.

"I'm not leaving," Joli announced matter-of-factly.

"Neither am I," Lajbi said, taking a stance next to Joli.

"You'll do as you are told," Momma said, almost as if she was telling us to clean the floor. "We must eat now," Momma said. I quickly began to stir the stew.

"I won't go," Joli said to herself.

"Can I take my tools?" Lajbi asked.

"I'm taking my doll," I heard Goldi say, "And I'm taking Pearl."

"Yes, you can take your doll and of course we are taking Pearl," Papa said.

"Come here Joli," Momma said. She held Joli in her arms.

"I won't go," Joli protested, holding back tears as Momma comforted her.

"You'll stay with your Momma," she said, "That's where you'll always be, no matter what happens or where you are."

Mendel came in; he was crying. "Papa says I have to leave my cat," Momma took him in her arms along with Joli.

"Yes love, but your cat will be happier here."

Pearl came trailing in and Momma pulled her into the big family hug, too. "I'm not crying," Goldie said. "Papa says we will all be safe," as the tears welled up in tough little Goldie's eyes.

"We will stay together," Momma said. Suddenly there were four brave and strong little warriors standing at my Momma's feet.

"Let's eat," Momma said. We all helped to get dinner on the table.

Later on, when Momma and I were in the kitchen alone, she patted me on the back. "We must be strong," she said to me. She stood erect and her eyes had a look of determination that only a mother could have. Her strength came from a place of love, tenderness, and devotion. I admired her for that. "You have always been a good daughter." She patted me on the back again. I hugged my Momma and she hugged back. In our moment of silence we both knew that there might not be many hugs left.

CHAPTER SEVEN

THE ROAD TO THE GHETTO

I WENT TO BED WITH AN ache in my heart and a lump in my throat. It was now obvious that we were going to be deported. No act of God nor man was going to stop the inevitable, as unreal as it seemed.

"Only an all-out blitz war by the Allies will save us," Papa had said at dinner; and we all knew that wasn't going to happen.

I laid awake, what felt like the entire night, thinking of Jacob. I wished more than anything I had told him one last time that I loved him, that we would survive and be together again when this was all over. I thought if I had just had the opportunity to have said the words out loud to him then it would be true. But then again, who was actually listening to anything we were saying?

The next day I sat on the front steps, trying to take in the final memories of the home that I loved so much when Mendel, Pearl and Yidel ran up to me in a panic.

"We will be the first to die," Mendel said. The words knocked me hard. I was speechless. How could he say that? He was right, but how could he have known that? "We won't be able to walk to Poland because we are too little."

"Who told you that?" I asked.

"I heard Momma and Papa talking about us," Mendel said.

I took him in my arms, wiped away his tears and kissed him.

"Don't you worry," I said. "I won't let anything happen to you. We will make it; the war will be over soon and we will be free again."

"Do you promise, Rifchu?" he implored.

"Yes, Mendel. I promise."

I had no idea how to keep such a promise, but I had no idea how not to make it. I held him tight against my chest. I couldn't believe this was really happening. It felt like a nightmare; being torn from our home, the risk of being murdered for just being Jewish was so outlandish. But it was happening.

Each day brought us more bad news. In the small town to the north all the Jews had been deported. In the town to the east, all the Jewish men had been rounded up and been forced into labor camps. It was happening so fast.

I woke up knowing that every day could be our last together. I spent my meals staring at the faces of my family, painting their pictures deep into my memory. I never wanted to forget them, the lines of their profiles, the colors of their eyes, the sound of their laugh. I didn't want to lose them altogether.

We were all sound asleep when the dreaded knock came. We had been waiting so long that our guard had dropped; we had started to feel safe like they would never come for us.

Papa was the first one to the door. We were all huddled in the living room waiting in silence. We knew what this meant. I strained to hear what the gendarmes were saying but their voices were muffled and they spoke quickly. Papa came back into the living room, his head hung low. The gendarmes had told him to prepare to leave the next morning. We were lucky; we were given warning and were to be relocated together.

Momma, Joli and I worked through the night to pack food for the family. Lajbi and Moshe packed a small amount of clothes and mementos. Morci helped Papa with the horse and wagon.

Just before dawn the next morning, on April 18, 1944, three gendarmes came to take us away from our home at gunpoint. We were ready and waiting in the kitchen for the knock but it was still startling. Somehow, I thought that it still may all a bad dream; it was so unreal. But there we were, being torn from our home.

We had tied our horse and wagon up outside the house, with our few necessities packed inside. The gendarmes allowed us to take it with us. Papa tugged at the reins of the horse and we were off. We left our home in silence. Before we got too far away, I turned and gave one last longing look at the home that I loved. Momma saw I was looking back, she put her hand on my shoulder, "Always look forward, my big girl."

With that our family of eleven was about to face the Holocaust.

The gendarmes lead us to a large group of Jews that were waiting along the Latorica River. The group consisted of Jewish families from neighboring towns as well as our own town. Once we merged with the group we were all told to march ahead.

Papa led the wagon. Morci walked next to him, Lajbi and Moshe trailed behind the wagon. My sisters and babies all stayed close together to me and Momma. I was so overwhelmed with anger and fear that tears were falling from my eyes.

"Wipe your face and walk proud, blondie," Momma said to me.

"I hate the Nazis!" I muttered under my breath.

Momma turned to see what I was referring to, "Be angry but do not hate. Hate is self-destructive," she responded.

I did my best to choke back my emotions. I wiped my eyes. I bite my lip but I still hated them.

As time went on the little ones began to get tired. Goldie held my hand. Momma carried baby Yidel. Soon Pearl and Mendel needed to climb up on the wagon.

"Follow close," Papa called as we began to drag.

The bridge across the river was jammed with deportees from the surrounding area. Those without wagons carried their belongings. There was a man in front of us who couldn't carry his load any longer. He collapsed to the ground. My brothers tried to help him up but a gendarme on horseback grabbed the bundle from the man and handed it to a gentile neighbor waiting for the opportunity to grab something.

"You should be able to get up now, Jew," the horseback gendarmes said to him.

Some of the gentile townspeople we knew were crying. A group of men that had made their living hauling Papa's lumber from the forest to Mukacheve ran out to bid a sad farewell to my Papa. There were others that were glad to see us go, they were more than happy to have a chance to take over Papa's business.

The gendarme's told us we were headed for the ghetto, the place where the Jews now lived. They had already stripped us of our civil rights and marked us with the yellow Star of David and now they were trapping us behind walls and barbwire? I could only imagine what was going to happen next. As we reached the gates of the ghetto, the gentiles grabbed at our horse's reins. They were trying to steal our horse and wagon. Papa tried to stop them. A fight broke out between the gentiles and my brothers and Papa. The gendarmes came and took the wagon from Papa at gunpoint. They gave the horse to the mayor, a one-time friend of Papa, and the wagon to another person waiting to steal from the Jews. The gentiles were pleased with their new possessions. The bystanders sat and laughed at us.

Pearl and Mendel cried from hunger and exhaustion. I put down the small bundle that I had been carrying so I could hold Mendel. Moshe and Lajbi walked next to Papa to keep the onlookers from snatching any more of our belongings. The government had ruled that a Jew couldn't own things, thus the gentiles weren't stealing from us. A Jew wasn't a citizen and had no rights; they were not people. It was up to us to protect our belongings and ourselves; no one was going to help us.

We arrived at the gate of the ghetto.

"Rest here for now...then you go on," they ordered.

But on to where?

CHAPTER EIGHT

THE MUKACHEVE GHETTO

THE FIRST STEP IN MAKING Hungary "Judenrein" (Jew Free) began by stripping Jews of their civil rights and citizenship. The government then forced us from our homes, corralling us into ghettos: empty warehouses, abandoned factories, brickyards, schools or synagogues. In some cases, the ghettos were nothing more than empty fields under the open sky.

While a small number of Jews were selected for labor service, in the end the majority of us were destined for a train ride to concentration camps. Only we didn't know that at the time.

We had marched all day from our village to the outskirts of Mukacheve, never given a break to stop for food or water. When we arrived at the ghetto in Mukacheve it had already reached the maximum capacity. We were forced to march on to Sajovit's Brick factory. A wealthy Jewish family had once owned the once prosperous brick factory. The factory was now a ghetto, surrounded by barbed wire, imprisoning not only the very family who used to own the factory but also thousands of other Jews. At each corner stood a tall watchtower. There were several soldiers with machine guns positioned in the towers overlooking the gate. The line halted when the camp was dead straight in front of us.

"Are they taking us to prison?" a young boy asked.

"No," his Momma said.

"But it looks like a prison," the boy replied.

"A ghetto is a place where they will protect us," a man said sarcastically.

"Protect us from what?" another child asked.

"It looks like a prison," the boy said again.

The gentiles stood along the road leading into the ghetto. They pushed through the soldiers to try to steal our small bundles.

"You won't need them where you are going," they said as they ripped the belongings from the hands of the Jews.

The Arrow Cross Nazis and Hungarian gendarmes didn't try to stop the stealing but did continue to try to rush us along, "Come on," they shouted. "Hurry up, Jews."

But the group did not move forward as ordered. When they got closer to the gates they began to panic. The front of the group turned and tried to run through the hoard of people standing behind them. Everyone tried to get out of the way but it was impossible, there were too many people packed to closely together. Chaos ensued. It was a stampede. Those who couldn't move fast enough were trampled. People were running and crawling, trying to save themselves. We were falling all over each other. Bodies twisting together legs and limbs were coiling together. Children separated from their parents. The soldiers laughed at our screams.

BANG! BANG! BANG!

Gun shots erupted from inside the gates. It silenced everyone, including the laughing soldiers. Six SS troopers marched out, machine guns pointing at us.

"Stay in line," a voice blared out over a loudspeaker. "This is your Hauptstrumfuhrer speaking. Get back in line and come through the gate. I repeat. Get back in line and come through the gate."

The SS troopers and Arrow Cross began pulling the fallen bodies up off the ground and tossing them into a standing position. The Nazis were screaming and kicking, doing whatever it took to get people up and in line. We listened. Did as we were told. There was no escaping. Families started to find each other and some sort of order ensued. And once satisfied, the SS troopers led us through the gates into the ghetto.

It was hard for me to see much around the crowd. I tried to get a sense of my surroundings but there were too many people. I finally was able to pick out the Hauptstrumfuhrer. He stood high on a wooden platform. Below him was a line of Hungarian gendarmes, machine guns slung over their shoulders. We were ordered to face him. There were several Jewish men with white armbands sewn around their tattered clothing translating the Hauptstrumfuhrer's orders into Yiddish. They were urging us to do as we were told.

"For your own good and safety do as he orders," one of the men with the white armband ordered.

Below the Hauptstrumfuhrer was a row of boxes. "I want you to voluntarily give up your currency, gold and silver, and all ammunition and guns. I warn each of you, there will be spot checks.

If valuables are found on you, there will be severe punishments," he said.

The Hauptstrumfuhrer was a young man with a square face and dark eyes. He wore a Nazi cap cocked to the side. It was a warm day but his tunic was buttoned up to his collar. He waited for someone in the group to come forward but no one did. Momma and Papa slowly pulled us towards the back of the group.

With a sweep of his hand, the Hauptstrumfuhrer signaled the gendarmes to move. They hurried through the group yanking out four young boys, four middle-aged men, and four old men. They grabbed them by their hair or their beards, pulled them forward and threw them to the ground. A brawny soldier, whip in hand, stepped out in front of the twelve individuals that were just pulled from the crowd.

People started to run to the boxes throwing down their gold, silver, wedding rings, anything that they had brought with them. If someone put silver in the box meant for gold they were smacked on the head or kicked.

One of the old men that was pulled from the crowd tried to sneak away. The gendarme grabbed him by his beard and announced he was to be shaved. The man began to plead with the gendarme, trying to tell him that he was a Hasidic Jew and it was part of his religion to have the beard. The gendarmes ignored his pleas instead pulling another Hasidic boy from the crowd to cut the man's beard. The boy told the gendarme that he could not cut the beard. The gendarme yelled for the Father of the boy to come forward.

"We will make the Jews understand the whip," the gendarme announced to the crowd.

The Hauptstrumfuhrer stood like a proud Papa over his men admiring the job they were doing and took the whip from the trooper. The man with the beard and the Father were to be beaten first. Their shirts were torn from their back. They both curled into tiny balls to protect themselves from the oncoming lashings. Everyone was shaking in fear. We had all learned the intended lesson – one acts out, we all can be punished. I held onto my Momma's hand praying someone or something would stop the man from being whipped.

The gendarmes swirled the leather thongs over their heads and with a smooth-practiced action they gathered momentum. The leathers swished in the air. The men's backs stiffened for the blows. The whips landed. It split down their backs, cutting their flesh. The men screamed. Drops of blood sprinkled the air drizzling the faces of those in the front row of the group.

The gendarme whipped the men two more times before the Haupstrumfuhrer put his hand in the air dismissing the men to the group. The poor bloodied men crawled back to the crowd, the flesh from their backs shredded.

However, the Nazis weren't finished teaching us all a lesson. The Father was dragged back out from the crowd and pulled to his feet. The gendarme handed him the whip.

"You must punish your son for not cutting the beard," he said to the man.

The Father's hands shook with anguish and pain. The gendarme pulled the boy's shirt off.

"Strike," the Hauptstrumfuhrer ordered.

"Strike," the trooper repeated.

The man stood frozen, staring at the clean white flesh on his sons back.

"Strike, please," one of the Jews with the white armband said, "or they will kill you both."

The man slowly brought the whip back. He swung it weakly in the air and struck his son. The boy screamed out in pain as blood droplets flew through the air.

"Harder," the trooper said. "You strike him harder or we will beat you both." The Father struck his son again. This time he hit him harder.

I started to cry out but Momma squeezed my hand tightly.

"What is happening?" Goldie asked. She couldn't see what was going on. Momma gave her a stern look that silenced her.

"Please, whoever has any gold or jewelry left, please give it to them," an anguished woman shouted.

The SS troopers and the Arrow Cross laughed at the fear that they caused. People ran forward with more valuables, hoping the beatings would stop.

"You see," the Hauptstrumfuhrer said, "I told you there was more." He smiled as the beatings continued.

I couldn't bear the screams. I covered my ears with my hands and closed my eyes. I felt a small hand touch my leg. I looked down. Mendel was staring up at me. "Don't worry, I'm here," he whispered.

I put my arms around his tiny neck and squeezed him. He hugged me back.

As the beatings ensued, one of Papa's friends spotted us in the group and pulled us away from the group. He brought us to Barrack 6, formerly a storage room for the bricks. He helped us find a corner where we could settle and then he helped us find work details.

Morci was made a medic in the infirmary. Moshe was put in charge of cleaning the areas outside the barracks. Lajbi and I were assigned to the kitchen. Papa remained in the barracks with Momma and the younger children. Joli wanted to work with me but Papa was worried that her headstrong disposition might get her into trouble and insisted she stay in the barrack. Momma didn't want me to work but Papa said that there were too many benefits of working in the kitchen. Kitchen workers received white armbands which gave a layer of protection from the Arrow Cross and Hungarians, and they also were able to get extra food.

Momma tried to make our corner of the barrack feel as much like 'our space' as possible. She spread out a blanket, unpacked our few remaining possessions, and tried to make it feel as comfortable as possible but the floor was damp, the roof leaked, and we were completely exposed to the elements.

Papa gathered in the center of the room with other men and prayed. They prayed for God to give them strength, to protect their families and save them from destruction. I'm sure there were others who prayed to sleep and never wake up.

We cuddled together in the corner of our new home. Goldie laid next to me on one side, her stomach growled from hunger but she didn't complain. Mendel snuggled next to me on my other side. "I'm cold," he said and hugged my waist. I kissed him and held him close until he finally fell asleep. I watched him in the darkness. My last thought before falling asleep was that I must keep my promise and protect him.

After the first few days, when the food the Jews brought with them had been consumed; potato and cabbage soup became the principal source of nourishment. This was always the main meal of the day. Bread was the only solid food that was given out. It was rationed to the amount of two slices per person per day. The competition for extra crumbs was fierce. Some resorted to thievery; others found ways to take advantage of slip-ups in the distribution system just to get a little extra.

Because of the primitive conditions, shortage of sanitary and bathing facilities, many people succumbed to dysentery, pneumonia, malnourishment, and other illnesses.

If the hardships and privations were not enough, we also had to endure the constant harsh treatment, cruelties and indignities meted out by the SS, Arrow Cross and Hungarian gendarmes. Hasidic Jews, easily identified by their black clothes, beards and peyote (side-locks), were objects of incessant punishment and brutalities.

Lajbi and I started work in the kitchen before dawn. It was my job to peel the potatoes. I liked my job, as tedious as it was, as long as I kept up with quota I was left alone. Before the sun came up I had already peeled a five-gallon bucket of potatoes.

At noon I got a break. I wandered out of the kitchen eating a potato. The white armband of the kitchen workers gave me a feeling of importance; the Arrow Cross would see me and leave me alone. In a daze, I walked aimlessly and didn't realize I was near the gate until I heard gunfire and saw a new group of Jews standing before the Hauptstrumfuhrer.

Though I had been in the ghetto only three weeks, it felt like old hand. The men in the new group had long beards and side-locks and were dressed in black. The women also were dressed in dark clothes. The men and women had been separated. Between the two groups stood a bearded, middle-age man with side-locks and two young boys. I knew I would regret witnessing the unfolding drama, yet I couldn't turn away.

The Hauptstrumfuhrer bellowed, "Unfortunately, we are not in the desert. It is too much trouble to make a sacrificial fire for the lamb." The guards got a great laugh from the Hauptstrumfuhrer's sadistic humor. "Make your choice as to which son shall be sacrificed. I will give you a few minutes to make your decision," he said as if he was being kind.

The bearded man fell to the ground and started praying. Bobbing his head and wailing upon deaf ears.

"It may help if you pray louder to your God. Maybe He will perform a miracle and produce a lamb to save your sons," the Hauptstrumfuhrer said laughing. The Hauptstrumfuhrer was referring to the biblical story of Abraham and his son Isaac, in which Abraham's faith in the Lord is tested. When Abraham shows God that he was willing to sacrifice Isaac in place of a burnt offering God spares Isaac.

Abraham's anguish over offering his son as a sacrifice was now, with horrendous mockery, about to be replayed by the depraved mind of the Hauptstrumfuhrer.

I was ready to scream, but the boys' Father screamed first, "No, I cannot make this choice. Let me be the sacrificial lamb. Please kill me."

"That was not one of the choices," the Hauptstrumfuhrer said, whereupon, from his position on the platform, he quickly pulled his pistol and shot the smaller child. The boy fell to the ground. Horrified, I ran to our corner of the barracks where Momma had to slap me back to a reality that I didn't want to return.

CHAPTER NINE

BROKEN GROUND

EACH MORNING, I WOKE HOURS before the sun. Momma would also wake up and help me get ready. She would hold a blanket around me while I would wash up and change into a clean dress. During the days Momma would wash our one change of clothes and hang it out on a line to dry. We would wear our clothes for several days before making the change. We had packed several pairs each but the gentiles took most during the raids when we entered the camps. But we couldn't complain, we were luckier than most. Many of the others near us didn't have a change or even a way to get clean. The single change of clothes made a huge difference.

Moshe had to be up even earlier than I did to clean the barracks. Typically, he would begin work in the middle of the night. He would sneak away before any of us woke. He would be done working before Lajbi and I were done. Moshe would come to check on us in the afternoon. He would also check on Morci in the infirmary.

We tried to check-in with each other several times throughout the day to make sure we were all okay and that none of us had been selected to be taken from the ghetto during our work shifts. It wasn't uncommon for people to go missing throughout the day. Some were taken into the city to work; many of the girls never came back from these trips. The Arrow Cross soldiers had been given a free hand to do whatever they liked with them.

As the days passed I made a point of avoiding where the Jews were processed. I would close my ears to the screams of the newcomers on my walk back to the barracks, and try to remember the sounds of home, but those sounds were fading.

★ ★ ★

As more and more Jews were brought into our ghetto, food became scarce. The rations were cut in half. People waited in line for hours for a cup of soup and a small piece of bread. I remained in the kitchen peeling potatoes. But I was given the added assignment of passing out food, which I hated. I couldn't bear the job of ladling soup, people begged for more, and if I were to give them more I would be beaten. So I gave them their half a ladle of soup and sent them on their way.

With the influx of so many people, the filth and the stench became unbearable. It was impossible to keep the ghetto clean. Moshe worked twelve to fourteen hours a day but there was no way to keep the refuse from piling up.

One afternoon, neither Moshe nor Morci came to the window. I waited and waited. They always came by to check on me at some point but neither of them had shown up. I was beginning to really worry about my brothers.

Through the back window, I saw several people running toward the fence behind our barracks. I hollered, "What's going on?"

An old man yelled back, "They are punishing the barrack cleaners. The SS said the barracks are like pigsties."

I dropped my peeling knife and rushed out the door following the man to the fence. As I came around the corner of the barracks, I saw that there were a large group of people gathered along the wired fence.

"Don't kill them!" someone yelled. I pushed through the crowd to where, through the tangled steel, I saw the barrack cleaners. They had been divided into two groups. There were twenty or so in each group. They were crawling on the hard ground strewn upon the broken bricks and rocks. The Arrow Cross soldiers had placed a brick in each of their hands, forcing them to hold them as they crawled on their elbows.

The Arrow Cross soldiers stood around monitoring the men. If one of the prisoners stopped crawling even for a moment the soldiers quickly let their batons fall upon their backs and then screamed at them to hurry. If they dropped a brick, a soldier picked it up and pushed it against their face bruising the flesh. One boy couldn't take it anymore and tried to run off. He was shot. Another boy passed out. His elbows bled.

"Move!" an Arrow Cross soldier ordered. The boy's eyes were closed. A solider set upon the boy, kicking and pummeling him.

"Don't kill him," a woman shouted. But the soldier continued. The boy never moved or made a sound. The blows kept raining on his face, chest, and groin. The boy opened his eyes to stare at the sky and he never moved again.

There was a trail of blood in the dirt that showed the path of the crawlers. Then I saw him. It was Moshe. Blood rolled down his forehead and into his eyes. An Arrow Cross was standing over him.

He was blindly moving on bloody elbows. He headed off course and the Arrow Cross hit him with a stick across the shoulder blades.

"My son!" I heard my Momma's voice yell. She was standing a short distance from me. "They're killing Moshe," she shouted. Papa and Morci were next to her. Neither had seen me. They were holding Momma back, trying to shield her from Moshe's torture.

"They are killing my son. Stop killing my son," she screamed. The Arrow Cross heard her and again struck Moshe on the shoulders.

A man with a white armband ran to Momma and told her to stop screaming. He told her that the more she screamed, the more Moshe would be struck. She refused to go. She clung to the fence and watched until Moshe collapsed. She gritted her teeth so she wouldn't scream. As much as it pained her, she would never leave him. As the boys collapsed, the Hauptstrumfuhrer signaled the medics to load them onto stretchers and take them to the dispensary. I ran to the barracks. I was supposed to go back to the kitchen but I didn't. I didn't care if the Nazis killed me.

"What are you doing here?" Papa asked.

"I'm not going back to the kitchen. The Nazis are murderers. They will kill us all," I screamed. I squeezed myself into a tight ball and screamed and screamed.

Momma pulled me upright and slapped me across the face, "No more of that," she said. "Go back to the kitchen. Your family needs you."

I held my face that stung from my Momma's slap. I didn't say a word. I just did an about face and did as I was told.

Moshe came back to us but I held onto my hatred. I knew that neither man nor God would help us.

CHAPTER TEN

THE LONG KISS GOODBYE

AS TIME WENT ON, my duties continued to grow. I was eventually trusted enough to carry food and water out to the trains that were moving the Jews out of Mukacheve. I would pack the maximum amount of food that was allotted for the maximum amount of people. Another worker and I would carry out the potatoes and water to the Jews packed in the train cars. The poor souls were crammed in so tight they could hardly breathe. They were so scared. They would ask me so many questions. They were desperate for answers. But I had none.

"Where are they taking us?" "Where are we now? Are we going to work? How much longer?" the Jews asked through the walls of the boxcars.

Hands would tug on my clothing from the train slots, pleading with me to give them something, anything – but I was as empty as they were. I couldn't provide them with anything but a bucket of potatoes and water, which was barely enough to feed everyone in the car. I would have to move quickly from car to car. I apologized to everyone for not being able to answer and wish everyone luck, it was all I could do especially with the guards yelling at me.

"Hurry, Hurry," they ordered us.

After I slid in each bucket the doors of the trains immediately slammed shut and the locks secured.

"We are suffocating," the people ranted. The Nazis had packed their Jewish prisoners less humanely than you would pack cattle. "Please leave the door open a little longer," they pleaded.

"Hurry! No talking!" the guards ordered.

The guards rolled the doors shut never making account that all appendages were back safely inside; the occasional finger would get caught between the car and the door. The sound of the bone cracking and the following shriek would send shivers down my spine.

***

The guards had told us that the people on the trains were being relocated to work in the factories in Germany. Some of the families in our ghetto volunteered to join them and were quickly taken away. These families thought that anything had to be better than the ghetto. They figured if they were allowed to work, the Nazis would appreciate their value and treat them better, so off they went into the boxcars.

Rumor in the ghetto was that the Russians were pushing the Germans back. We figured that the Germans were rounding up the Jews to fill the labor shortage in the Third Reich's war factories.

Momma and Papa had discussed, and agreed it was better to wait. "The unknown may be worse," Papa said.

"We are here together," Momma said, holding Yidel.

Pearl's head rested on Momma's lap. We were all here together, in our tiny corner of the universe, safe, under the watchful eye of Momma and that was good enough for her.

***

Each day as I peeled potatoes, I would try not to think about the disparity of my reality. I focused on peeling as fast as I could knowing that the more potatoes I peeled meant the more nourishment there was for the starving. When a train came through or left from the station my work partner and I rushed out to meet all the departing cars. It was up to us to meet the trains on time. If we missed a train, that train didn't get food. The Nazis had given us our orders and the schedules. We had been left up to our own accord to get the food to the trains. This was most likely due to the fact that the Nazis didn't really care if the Jews got fed or not. I had made sure that that I was always prompt and followed the rules, over time, my movements had become relatively unsupervised around the rail tracks.

With all of my time peeling and day dreaming, I began to speculate that it could just be possible that Jacob could have been brought to one of the ghettos near us and that one day he would pass through on one of the boxcars. I became determined to find him and finally get to say my last good-bye. As the guards stood-by, I would run from boxcar to boxcar with the buckets. But when they turned their backs I would asked for 'Jacob Polak' in Czech, Hungarian, Yiddish, and Ukrainian: "Any Jews from Chynadiyovo? Is Jacob Polak among you?"

One day, after days and weeks of asking I got a response from a man who used to live in Chynadiyovo, "Girl. Girl. Jacob and his family were in the ghetto with me. I assume he will be transported soon."

"Where is he going to?" I asked.

"I don't know. All we were told is that we were going to work and that the Jews were needed to help with the war efforts," he responded.

"Thank you. Thank you," I told him holding his hand through the slits.

"Don't believe that," a man from the boxcar yelled. "Whatever you do, don't let them get you onto the train." I quickly left the train because the Arrow Cross guard was walking toward me.

The days continued on, and as they did I continued to I asked for Jacob Polak. "He is here," a voice called from the boxcar. My heart stopped. *Was it really possible?* I couldn't breathe. When the door opened, Jacob pushed through the sea of bodies to take the bucket from me. As he grabbed the bucket from my hands the door began to close, our only touch was the brief exchange of the bucket switching between our hands. I felt my entire body tingle as his hand gently brushed against mine. "Rifchu," he said with a sad smile. I wasn't able to say anything. I just stared at him. So skinny. So sad. I knew that couldn't be my only interaction with him. I needed a real good-bye.

"Wait, I will ask the Hungarian guard to let you off the train for a moment," I said as the door was closing.

"Don't do it," Jacob said, "You are taking a risk. I am afraid he could hurt you," he said through the slots.

"He seems to have a kind face," I said, looking at the nearest guard.

The guards were two cattle cars away taking pictures of the prisoners in the trains. I approached him slowly. "Good afternoon," I said in Hungarian. "May I ask for a special favor?"

"What kind of favor do you need?"

"My friend is in one of the cars. Could you let him out for just a few minutes, please?" I asked.

The guard looked at me curiously and then nodded, "You have a few minutes. Have a moment of happiness," the guard said.

The guard walked back to the car with me and opened the door.

"Thank you, sir," Jacob said, as he jumped down from the cattle car.

I ran into his arms. I melted into him when our bodies met and his arms wrapped around me. I felt his gentle lips on mine. Our tears mingled like two streams merging into one.

"This nightmare won't last forever, Rifchu. The Russian army is near the border."

"I fear this won't end soon enough for us. I can't take the cruelty from the Arrow Cross and the children crying from hunger. I can't listen to the older people praying for their lives to end. People are dying every day."

From the corner of my eye, I saw the guard photographing us but I didn't care. Perhaps that was his reason for letting us out. All I knew was that I was here with Jacob, if just for a moment. Even if it was possibly a dream.

"I know it is hard to watch the suffering. You must not give up. You must not let them break you. I love you. Promise me you won't give up," he said.

"I love you, too. But all I can promise you is that I will do my best."

I felt his heart against my heart as he held me tightly. He kissed me on each cheek.

"You must not forget I love you. We will meet after the war," he told me.

The locomotive whistled. It startled me.

"I guess it is time," he said.

Jacob crawled back into the train car and blew me one more kiss as the doors slammed shut. I watched the train pulled away from the station and stood in the same spot until it was out of sight. When I turned back towards the ghetto I realized that I was alone. My kitchen partner was gone and the guards had left me there. Now, I was really unsure if I was dreaming or not. *Had they forgotten about me? Was the one guard so into taking pictures he forgot to stand watch?* Either way, there I was, staring freedom smack dab in the face. It was just past the train tracks. I felt like I was looking at a painting. The tracks were a divide; purgatory and paradise. Fields of yellow wildflowers so thick and full like a deep wool carpet. I could almost smell the aroma. I wanted to run. I thought about it. I wanted to lay down in the flowers and hide in the mess of their blossoms and petals through summer. I wanted to turn into a bird and fly away. I got ready to run to freedom but I couldn't move. I stood there. *What would my parents think?* They would be devastated. They would never know what happened to me. Momma said we should stick together and that whatever happened would happen to everyone.

I turned around and went back to the kitchen and continued peeling potatoes.

CHAPTER ELEVEN

GO TO THE RIGHT

T HE EARLY HOURS OF May 1944 were dark and still. The clouds had swallowed up the moon and stars. I lay awake in the darkness on the hard floor of the ghetto staring out the open walls searching for the sounds of the waterwheel in my head but all the darkness brought me was the sounds of war cannon fire from the Russian front many miles to the east.

Momma had been happy each night that we had survived the day without being selected to get on the train. She had hoped that the longer we were in the ghetto, the more chance there was that the Russians would arrive in time to free us. But each night, as the sounds of war filled the darkness, it was apparent that the Russians were not going to come in time. As it turned out, we were on the last train to leave the ghetto.

It was May 19, 1944, a week before the happy spring festival of Shavuot. We should have been baking dairy cakes and decorating the house with flowers. But this festival season, I was to celebrate by staring at the moon and stars through the space between the slats of a cattle car.

To get us to enter the boxcars, the guards cajoled us, and

when this did not work we were pushed and kicked and beaten like we were disobedient livestock. The light of the moon dimly lit the figures of my family. In all, there were perhaps sixty people jammed inside the car. We had no room to stretch out our legs. We sat with our knees bent into our chins. To use the limited room to the best advantage, we sat with our backs against one another or the sides of the car.

Yidel was in Momma's arms, not crying like most of the other babies. His blue eyes twinkled in the glow of the eerie night. In the moonlight, Momma had a look of utter confusion on her face. I watched as the waves of anxiety ran over her. She had been so calm during past maelstroms, always optimistic, but now crammed in the cattle car, it was apparent that the Nazis had finally squashed the last bit of hope she had. It crushed me. She was such a gentle, loving soul who never harmed any one, a person after God's own heart. And now she found herself and her family degraded, helpless and captive.

A harsh bang followed by the clang of an iron bar jarred and with that the boxcar door sealed us in. It had become a familiar sound to me during my time bringing food out to the cars, yet it sounded so different being trapped inside. There was even less air and light with the doors shut. The train began to rumble and the boxcars banged into one another with a harsh force. The jolt spilled us over, and we toppled onto one another. The children and babies screamed and many old people yelped out in pain from the force.

Where were we bound, no one knew. It was hot inside the car. We all wheezed and puffed into one another's faces. A kind of lethargy and resignation to an unknown fate set in. Finally, a man nearby said, "If they would let us work they would see we can be useful." His remark addressed no one in particular and went unanswered.

The boxcar jostled onward for days. The car was unbearably hot, and only the few who took up positions in the front of the car and along the sides could feel the thin streams of air that sifted through the openings of the slats. We used our few items of clothing as cushions against the hardness of the floorboards.

By the time we had left the ghetto food was scarce. Thus, we had only been given a half a bucket of potatoes and a bucket of water when we got on the train. When we finished eating the potatoes, the empty bucket was used for excrement. We had not been given any food for the second day. Momma had baked mandal bread before we left our home. Thankfully, this cookie-like bread stayed edible for months. After the potatoes were gone, she doled out pieces of the cookie, not to just our family but also to those nearby.

Before long, the stench from urine, feces, vomit, and sweat added to our extreme discomfort. We were so close to one another that some would fail to reach the bucket and would accidently vomit on the person next to them. This and the other miseries provoked loud arguments between everyone.

We hadn't moved our limbs for twenty-four hours. We sat knees to chin on the rattling floorboards. Our stomachs were empty as the water bucket. At least there was nothing left to vomit-up. Only the wheels and coupling joints of the cars were heard. We had fallen into an eerie silence. Exhaustion, depression, and despair filled the car. I closed my eyes and tried to drift my mind back to the sound of the waterwheel but it was gone.

On the third day the train stopped. The doors slid open. Sunlight splashed into the car and the fresh air rushed in. Our bodies rose as wilted flowers do in a refreshing rain. I sat up trying to ascend above the others' heads to breathe in the air.

Shouting came from outside the door: "Out with the pot! Don't you want some food, Jews?" A man jumped down and emptied the buckets of waste. We were given a fresh bucket of water.

We heard knocking on the sides of the car; it was the locals offering to trade bread for gold pieces. "Hurry, give it to me. You won't need gold where you are going. In Auschwitz you will be forced to give up everything, including your clothing. Most of you will be killed. Why not buy some food now?"

No exchanges were made. No one believed they would give us bread. I don't think anyone believed that we were going to be killed, not that we spoke about it. The locals moved on to another car and the door to our car was slammed shut. The train stopped several more times over a period that seemed to last an eternity; each stop brought additional chaos outside the car and greater misery inside the car.

As the train began to move, the cars clanged together, we were jolted forward rocking into one another like cheap cargo. I dimly saw the face of Moshe. His hands were folded around his legs, his chin resting on his knees. In outline, his face had grim determination. Morci and Lajbi had the same resolve to survive all this on their faces, a look of anger and bravery.

It made sense to believe that we were bound for a labor camp. After all, we had learned of Jews working in factories and living in guarded ghettos. It also seemed sensible to think that since the Nazis were losing the war they would need more and more slave workers. *Why should they go on slaughtering when so many Jews could be pressed into servicing the war efforts?* We held onto the hope that our still healthy bodies might save us while forced to work the German factories. At least that's what Momma thought; she would not believe that they would kill us all. I wanted to believe Momma but somewhere deep in my heart I feared that the locals' mutterings were true and that my family and I would die.

Sitting in the boxcar, I remembered Morci telling me that Hitler had once said that nature is cruel; therefore man must be cruel. And since Hitler didn't seem to mind sending the cream of German society into hell and war, he certainly wouldn't give a damn about the death of millions of Jews.

On the fourth night, May 22, 1944, the train ground to a final stop. The doors rolled open. Huge searchlights illuminated the car, blinding me. I couldn't make out much of what was ahead. All I could see were the black silhouettes of soldiers and rifles.

An SS officer came up to the car, screaming for us to get down. Our car began to empty. I started to walk forward to the edge of the boxcar. Papa said something to me but I couldn't hear him. Everything was so loud. The screams of the soldiers and the crowd were over bearing. My head was roaring and spinning with sounds.

A little boy from our car had gotten separated from his parents and was about to be trampled. Morci jumped down to pull him out of the way of the running crowd. I was ready to jump out but Momma grabbed my shoulder and spoke directly into my ear, "Let's not rush. Let's watch what is happening."

"Heraus! Heraus! Schneller!" "Out, out faster," the SS yelled.

I am not sure why I jumped, but I did. I didn't realize how high off the ground the cattle car was; I couldn't break my fall and fell face first into the uneven rocky surface. At the same time, I came crashing down, a quick sharp blow came reigning downward on my back. I took a deep inhale to try to catch my breath.

"Get up, Jew," a guard ordered.

As I lifted myself to my feet, I was starting to breathe normally but to my horror the air smelled horrible but not the same way as it did in the cattle car. The smell was familiar. I took another deep breath: burnt mutton. I hated when my grandma would make mutton, the stench always made me sick. I looked around, I couldn't figure out where the smell was coming from. What I didn't know yet was that stench was that of burning human flesh and it was all around, billowing from the five concrete chimneys.

The searchlights cut across the dark sky. They lit up the ground so bright that I could have found a needle on the ground. "Out Jews. Out. Get in a line. Leave everything behind." All around, soldiers were equipped with machine guns, bayonets and side arms.

My family had made it off the boxcar and was being herded nearby. I ran to join them. Behind me, back at the train, men in blue and white uniforms were jumping in and out of each train car throwing out whatever items we left behind.

I wobbled to keep my balance as needles of pain shot through my legs. We were pushed and shoved together. Papa, Moshe, Morci and Lajbi stood together in front of me. Papa turned to say something, I could see his mouth moving but I could not hear what he was saying. Momma held Yidel, Pearl and Mendel held onto her dress and Goldie stood with Joli. I think I tried to scream but if something came out no one could hear it, not even me.

A few people broke ranks and ran to the disabled and sick and tried to save them but the SS beat and pushed them back into line. The chaos and screaming rose as clubs and rifle butts were used to prod us along. The line hardly moved as people from the other boxcars were pushed into the line. A cloud of ominous gray smoke hovered over all of our heads.

Families were bidding tearful final good-byes and well wishes. Husbands and wives were holding on to each other until they were ripped apart. Mothers and daughters and Fathers and sons held on to each other for dear lives, literally.

The line shuffled forward. Momma held Yidel in her arms and Pearl's hand. I held Mendel and Goldie's hand and Joli walked beside me. As we walked the voice from the loudspeaker was in sharp contrast to the shouting of the guards. The voice was reassuring, repeating the same words over and over: "Keep moving forward. You will be given food and shelter. Don't be alarmed. Keep moving forward."

Yidel announced that he was hungry by letting out a loud wail. Momma reached into her pocket for some cookies to calm him but she realized that she had left the bag on the train. "The bag, get the cookie bag! He must have something to eat," she said to me.

I was so scared, "Please, send one of the boys!" I begged.

But when we looked around we saw that they were gone, they were all gone! My brothers and Papa had been pulled out of line by the SS!

My Mommas was so panicked. I didn't want to upset her so I decided to just...run. We were still within sight of our boxcar so I thought I had a chance. I noticed that the SS had moved on while the crew of four men in the blue and white uniforms were cleaning out our car. As I started to climb into the car, the hand of a skeleton reached out from the shadow and grabbed my arm. I gasped in fear.

It was one of the men cleaning the cars. He was so skinny. All I could see were his deep-set eyes and his teeth. His skin hung off him like he was wearing a suit that was too big.

"I need to get a few crumbs of food for my baby brother," I said, pointing to my Momma and the kids.

He interrupted me with a wave of his hand. "Go back to the line," he said hoarsely, "Tell your Momma to put the baby down and go with you to the right. Remember, go to the right, for only then will you have a chance to survive."

I tried to pull away but he held on to me and said, "Tell your Momma what I said. On the left are the gas chambers. That smell is burning hair and flesh. You're in Auschwitz. Don't touch the fences; they are electrified. This is the end of the line. The only way out is through the chimney."

As I turned to look at the smoke billowing from the massive cement tubes into the sky the old man pushed me off away from the train.

"What do you mean, this is Auschwitz?" I said, more asking myself. Then I remembered what the gentiles at one of our train stops had told us as they tried to trade food for jewelry. No one had believed them when they taunted us and told us that we were going to be killed. Now all the rumors that we had heard in our village and the various transit camps were confirmed, we were at a death camp.

I ran straight back to my family. I told my Momma what I had been told. I told her that, no matter what, I was not leaving her and that we would die together. She tried to quiet me. I knew that we were going to die, even if we were chosen for labor.

All the while, the line moved ever closer to the parting point, the point of selection.

As we approached the head of the line, SS men and women were pulling the very old and very young from the line and throwing them to the left. In a severe tone of voice, my Momma ordered me, "Take Goldie and Joli and push yourselves to the right."

"I won't go, Momma!" I cried. "I won't go without you! Momma, come with us, you can't save the babies! You must believe me! Come with us, come with us!" I yelled.

Mendel yelled at me, "You promised to take care of me, Rifchu. You Promised!"

I ignored his plea. There was nothing I could do to save him. I hadn't expected this. *Who could have expected this?* I needed my Momma, too. I clung to her more fiercely. She tried to push me away and loosen my grip. But I wouldn't let her go.

A soldier grabbed a young baby from its Mother's arms. Holding the baby by its feet, he struck it with a bayonet. The baby shrieked once. The Mother threw herself at the soldier and was then shot. The soldiers all laughed. Enraged, some of the prisoners broke from the line to attack the soldiers with their bare fists. They were gunned down.

Momma pushed me again, "I must go with the little ones.

Someone must. I can't let them die alone. Go to the right with Goldi and Joli. You must live. They cannot kill us all. Promise me you will look after yourself and the others."

I continued to beg her but she broke free from my hold. I tried to pull the little ones off of her. They were crying but I wasn't going to lose my Momma. I needed her. She managed to pull me off of her and she gave me a hard push to the right, "Promise me, my big brave girl." Just as the last word left her mouth, an SS pulled her, Mendel, Pearl and Yidel to the left.

It was all I could do to whimper out, "I promise you, Momma."

I found myself on the ground having fallen across the tracks. As I began to push myself up to a standing position, a tall man SS man was standing over me. His uniform was covered in decorations. Although I did not know it then, it was the "Angel of Death" himself, Dr. Mengele. As I looked him over he kicked me hard in my gut, again I lost my breath.

As I made it to an upright position, I had to shake off the dizziness and fear. I heard a woman's voice calling. I thought it was Momma calling to me, reminding me to take care of Goldie and Joli. But Momma was no longer in sight. My body started to heave but before I could cry an SS officer pushed me forward to join a group of older children and women. *Where were Goldie and Joli? Where were my brothers and Papa? And where was my Momma?*

As I came out of my riot of thoughts, I realized that I was walking to the right.

CHAPTER TWELVE

LUCKY TO BE ALIVE

S TANDING IN THE NAZI'S ASSEMBLY line of death was no time for philosophical thoughts. Staying alive was the name of the game. Protecting Goldie and Joli shaped my every thought and effort. I needed to find them.

While being marched along by the guards, my attention kept shifting back to Momma, Yidel, Mendel and Pearl. I could not accept that they were just a few steps from the gas chamber and the crematorium. Suddenly, I felt a tiny hand in mine. I looked down and there was Goldie. She had found me. I was relieved but unable to even acknowledge her. She was crying, but I hardly heard her between the commotion in the line and in my head. I was so glad she was back with me but at that moment I was numb.

"Rifchu, are you alright?" Goldie asked, trying to interrupt my thoughts.

I pretended not to hear. I had no idea how to answer her and I was terrified of whatever question she may have next. She was counting on me to be strong, like at home, when she was frightened. But I was as frightened as she was.

"Where are they taking us? Are they going to kill us? Where is Momma?" she asked.

How could I answer her?

"We need to find Joli," I told Goldie, hoping that would change the subject. Momma had told me to take care of her, too; Momma must have seen her going to the right.

Trapped beyond the barbwire fences were thousands of women, I pointed towards them, "Look Goldie. Here is your answer. Look at them. If they are alive, we can stay alive, too," I told Goldie. Goldie gave my hand a squeeze. The women behind the electric fences may have been alive but they appeared to be like the undead: hollow-eyed, hairless zombies dressed in rags. *Was that the best we could hope for at this point?*

"Rifchu, talk to me!" Goldie cried as she shook my hand.

"I don't know what is going to be but I promise that we will be together. That's what counts. Let's go find Joli," I said.

If there was ever a place that God ignored it was Auschwitz. He was nowhere to be found in the death camps. To enter Auschwitz was to pass into the devil's domain. Those not marched into the gas chambers witnessed the devil's doings. *If God were involved in the selection process, why would He not allow mothers and innocent children to live?* While such thoughts played out in my mind, I again saw my Momma's distorted face as she pushed me to the right. Tears were in her eyes, but behind her eyes was a woman of ruthless determination. She had decided to die with her babies. She turned the idea of "survival at all costs" on its head. Her love for her children was so great that she hoped to give them even one more half-hour of comfort and to help them die. She was just forty-two-years old and could easily have been selected for labor.

Goldie's big doe eyes stared up at me desperately pleading me for answers. She was hardly eleven-years-old. I pushed the hair back from her dirty face and wiped the tears from her eyes with my hands. Her sweet face looked so much like little Mendel's. I had failed him so epically. *Did I really try to pull Momma away from him?* Did this little boy yell, "You promised to take care of me!?" *If the time of choosing came again would I break my promise to Goldie just as I had to Mendel? And, what about Joli?* She was almost sixteen, just about two years younger than me and two inches taller. *How would I control her?*

As we continued to move forward and merge from a crowd into a line, order started to ensue. In the midst of the crowd I spotted Joli's golden locks. I called out to her. It took several times but she finally heard me. I held on tightly to Goldie's hand as I ducked to her level so we could serpentine our way upwards in the line towards Joli.

"Thank God," Joli said. We hugged and moved on in the line together.

We came to a sudden halt. "Stay in line and wait your turn," a guard screamed.

In front of us stood a large brick building and several wooden barracks. I repeated Momma's instructions the girls: "Listen to me! Momma made me in charge of your safety. You will need to help me. We must stay together. Okay? It's very important that we stay together as much as possible." They both nodded. Too scared to disagree even if they wanted to.

Vermin and rats had a natural home in Auschwitz. They were everywhere. What grass grew quickly disappeared into the mouths of the starving, leaving the grounds brown and baron.

Those of us from rural villages knew that the hardscrabble that we were walking on would become either ankle-deep mud or tundra like concrete during the winter. We headed down a hard cinder road for processing where we would be transformed from individuals with families and hopes and dreams into fully de-graded prisoners indistinguishable from thousands of others. I couldn't help but wonder how long it would be before we would look like the cadavers who had called to us from the fence.

Black smoke spewed from a building not far from us, the air smelled of burnt hair. "Rifchu, where is that screaming coming from?" Joli asked. I hadn't even noticed.

"Just worry about you," I told her.

As we entered the camp, armed SS female guards pushed the group we were with forward. Skull insignias and swastikas adorned their green uniforms. They carried leather truncheons, swishing them through the air as they walked by each of us. I shielded Goldie and the truncheon landed across my back. It felt like a steel rod had cut through my skin and sent shock waves up my spine. Tears began to flow down Goldie's face. As much as I wanted to scream out in pain, I had to hold it back, hold back the tears. "I'm alright," I told her as I tried to straighten up. I had my fair share of beatings for one day but I didn't have a choice but to continue on.

When it was finally our turn to enter the brick building, the guards ordered us to get undressed and to leave our clothing be-hind. "Hold your shoes only and move forward. Blonds lineup in the first two rows; brunettes in the next two, then redheads and then black haired girls."

As we stood in line we found out what the screaming was

about; not everyone at this point was going to live. The very young were immediately being taken to the crematorium. I instructed the girls to lie about their ages if asked. Goldie was to say that she was twelve and a half; Joli was to say she was seventeen, and I would say I was nineteen. At the same time, I decided to change my name. My Momma had always hated my name and had always refused to call me by my name; she referred to me as her big girl or blondie. She had wanted to name me after her Mother but Papa had gone to the synagogue and named me Sura Rifka anyway. Now that Momma was dead I decided at the moment that no one would ever call me Sura Rifka or Rifchu (my nickname) again. My name would be Edita, meaning spoils of war, because that is what we had become. I told my sisters of my name change. While they gave me a strange look, nothing could come as a surprise given the situation.

"Ober schneller" (faster), shrieked the SS women. They urged us in multiple languages to obey and do as we were ordered. We were also instructed to not speak to each other during processing.

As we stood naked, I hugged Goldie and Joli. "I am the oldest, therefore I am in charge. I promise I will do my best to shelter you." Even as I spoke the words I questioned my resolve. I wondered if this was what my Momma wanted from me. We pressed forward.

Chairs lined the large dimly lit room. Standing by each chair was a woman with a tattoo number along their forearm. They were armed with large shears. They were quickly and expertly removing the hair off the heads of the new prisoners. I now understood the orders we had been given.

"They are dividing us up by hair color. Joli, you have blond hair you have to go to the left, I will be right behind you. Goldie, you have to go to the second line with all the other girls with brown hair. Be brave, it will be alright."

"I don't want to go," whimpered Goldie.

"So what if we look like those crazies we saw lined up outside? Our hair will grow back! Don't worry." I tried to reassure her with my little pep talk but I was also shaking and needed to buck up. But Goldie wouldn't leave my side. I figured if the SS didn't force her away from me, I would stay with her as long as I could.

From all corners of the room, SS men and women poked at us with every form of prod one can think of. Men in civilian clothes came and went giving hurried orders. "Move swine," a large SS woman shouted. The women with the shears worked speedily, especially when the SS stood by. The shears must have been worn because they seemed to tear out more hair than they cut, causing gashes along the scalps.

It was Joli's turn in a chair next. She tried to cover her body with her arms and shoes. Tears rolled down her face. I had rarely seen Joli cry; she was always the tough one growing up.

Then it was my turn. The shears nicked my scalp. I winced in pain, but held back as much as I could for Goldie, whose hand was still locked in mine. I walked Goldie to the woman who was going to cut her hair. We had to pass several male SS Officers. I was so ashamed that I could not cover my body. I had never been completely undressed in front of a man, not even a doctor. My legs shook.

"Move on. Swine," the SS ordered.

We waited in the line for Goldie's hair to be sheared. The woman with the shear called out: "Next." I had to push Goldie forward, her tiny naked body frozen in place.

"It will be okay," I whispered to her.

As I waited for her I felt a jabbing finger on my shoulder. It was the SS woman. She pointed at my black patent leather shoes and ordered me to give them up. Behind her stood a woman in a stripped uniform, she handed me a pair of wooden clogs. My heart dropped. The shoes were the last of my belongings from home. Without protest, I gave the woman my shoes and took the wooden clogs.

I went back to stand in support of Goldie. The dull shears moved over Goldie's head. Her small thin body heaved with sobs. In a voice slightly above a whisper I pleaded to the shearer to leave a little hair on Goldie's head. When the SS woman wasn't looking, the shearer spoke to me, never looking in my direction, "The young girl on my right, with the hair, has been selected by a blockhova (female inmate supervisor) to be her pet. She'll be safe until the blockhova tires of her. Then she goes to the SS for experiments or to the gas chamber. We don't get children on this side of the camp. You and your sister escaped this time but the place you are going has daily selections. Only the Jews that have been here for a long time and that have been chosen to be prison staff have hair and tattoos." She pointed to the blue numbers on her arm, "It means that sometimes I get extra rations, and that I am used to help destroy other Jews. This is Auschwitz II- Birkenau, there is no special treatment for anyone." She spoke rapidly. She was inexplicably bold to have poured out such information for it was surely dangerous to do so. "And, you are headed for

Lager C. That is worst barrack here. It's the reserve cattle pen for Dr. Mengele, the 'Angel of Death'".

"Reserved for what?" I demanded.

"The crematoriums, experiments, sex, whatever they need bodies for. They even use bodies for soap. Don't envy my job. The Germans will kill us all in time." She kept cutting Goldie's hair. "But don't worry about the soap. You're too thin for soap. They'll use you for a lampshade."

The woman's last words were a well-intentioned warning: "Get out of Lager C as fast as you can and whatever you do avoid special selections!"

A voice shouted: "Out, swine!"

The next stop was a place they called the sauna. It was a huge wet room used for communal cleansing. While we waited, I came to the conclusion that here, nothing existed. The last thing that gives life meaning and value was also taken from us, our name. Our identities were meaningless, we hadn't even been given a tattoo like the earlier Jews or the workers. Here, we were not even a number.

Jolie, Goldie and I stood huddled next to one another, holding hands. Others in the sauna called the names of relatives and friends, able to recognize them only by voice in the multitude of naked bodies pressed together.

"Place your shoes along the wall, filthy swine. You will have a shower," the SS yelled.

The doors slammed shut. There was more screaming and a lot of praying. As we stood body-to-body, how could any of us know that this was really a shower? It was natural to think that the spigots in the ceiling could be gas outlets. This was

Auschwitz II-Birkeneu. A small trickle of brown, ice-cold water came from the ceiling. What little murky water there was seemed wonderfully refreshing. But we were hardly wet when the water stopped flowing and were ordered to vacate. It was nothing more than a tease. Hardly enough to clean off the vomit and feces from the train ride.

We were marched out of the building, wet and naked. We entered another barrack. There, staff prisoners threw clothes at us. I got a black cotton dress with short sleeves; it was two sizes too big. Joli got a gray wool dress with long sleeves; it fit her perfectly. Goldie received a long short sleeve brown dress that she had to hold up when she walked. It was ridiculous. We burst out laughing. It was the first bit of comic relief we had in weeks. We laughed so hard that tears began to stream down our faces. Joli suddenly stopped laughing.

"Edita," Joli said, as the color drained from her face. She was pointing out the window. I was terrified to look. I followed her finger. Outside the window was a large group of men. The men had obviously been processed in the same way we had been. Their heads were shaved and they had been given shabby new clothes to wear. But, what Joli was really pointing at was the sight of Papa and our three brothers. I have no idea how she saw them, but she did.

What was even more astonishing was that Papa looked toward the window where we were standing and he saw us - a gift from Momma. He approached the window. "Where is Momma?" he asked.

I whispered so my sisters couldn't hear me, "She went to the gas chamber."

The awful impact of my answer etched his face. All along he had thought that Momma, who was strong and healthy, would be safe, at least for now. He should have known that known that Momma would never leave the little ones to die alone.

It was difficult to speak through the window and the commotion. Papa knew that whatever he said to me now may be his last words. He didn't know if they should be words of wisdom or final goodbyes. He urged us to be aware of all dangers for they were everywhere. He said to trust no one except each other. To stick together at all costs. He started to tell us how much he loved us and he would see us soon but he then broke from his salutations and started yelling for me to run. Before I could turn, a blow landed near my ear sending me flying back into the line of prisoners. *Again!* Next thing I knew, Joli and Goldie were helping me to stand up and my Papa and brothers were gone.

CHAPTER THIRTEEN

LAGER C, BLOCK 24

WE WERE MARCHED, FIVE ABREAST, through Auschwitz II- Birkenau until we came to an electrified gate with a sign: LAGER C. Inside we were divided into groups, 1000 women per block. An SS woman with blond hair, immaculate uniform, buttons polished and boots shining marched us in. She conducted her new charges in an arrogant way occasionally looking up to stare us down like a lion would its prey. Her demeanor made it known that her sidearm pistol was not merely an accessory to the uniform.

Standing beside the SS guard, was an old, grey haired woman, the Blockhova. The young unshorn girl I had seen earlier accompanied the old woman. This older woman held the girl's hand. She glanced down at the little girl as though to assure her that she was superior to the others in the ranks and could protect her. Another SS woman with tied back brown hair and a pretty scarf counted us and assigned us Block numbers. Joli, Goldie and I were assigned to Block 24, located at the far end of Lager C.

"Halt!" the SS officer shouted before we started left for our block. Those that did not understand German did not halt and were struck with a rubber hose. "I am your Hauptstrumfuhrer. I will introduce you to your Blockova, to whom you will address as Frau Aufseherin. You will take your orders from her. She will report to me if any of you get out of hand. Do as she commands."

Each group was assigned a Blockova. The Blockhova was a Jewish woman given protection and power by the Nazis in return for basically turning on her own people. We headed towards our new home, Lager C – Block 24. Lager C was between the family camp, (primarily made up of Czechoslovakian's,) and the men's camp. On the other side of the men's camp was the gypsy camp. All of the camps were divided by barbwire fences. Running north of all of the Lagers was the train tracks. Block 24 was located at southern most point of Lager C.

The Blockova addressed us: "I hope you understand completely that I am in charge of you. You are my animals and I expect all of you to obey me. You are not to address me unless I give you permission."

Our Blockova was a woman named Ruzena Palakova. She had a number tattooed on her arm and hair on her head. Her face was cruel and she carried a stick that she flourished as she spoke. "If you disobey me, I will not hesitate to use force to keep you in line. Don't let things get to that point." She paced before us as she continued to impress upon her authority and intentions.

"I shall select twenty-four women as kapos. They will help me, and for this they will receive extra rations and have a registration number that will exclude them from daily selections," our Blockhova continued.

I thought that having a number must be a good thing. But, I knew if I left Goldie that she couldn't survive the days on her own.

Thus that thought quickly passed. What I needed to worry about was the daily selections. *What could we possibly be selected for?*

She went on to tell us about Lager C's daily routines, "There will be 'Zum Appell' (roll call) in each block twice a day. The first roll call will be begin at 4:00 am. When you hear the second whistle you will walk out to the area next to the block. When everyone has been accounted for you can return to your bunk. At this time, you will be given food. Each bunk of ten women will receive a pot of soup to share. At 3:00 p.m. you will again line up for roll call. After the completion of this roll call, you will receive a loaf of bread for each row to share between you. After the working parties are accounted for, you will be dismissed or taken to the toilet before returning to the barracks for the night. I will now assign you to a bunk."

She counted off ten girls and pointed to a three-tiered bunk. The girls hurried to claim the best spots in the bunk. We were ordered to arrange ourselves head to toe so that all our bodies would fit. The bunks were old splintering wooden planks.

We got a top bunk at the very back at the barrack. There was little air on the third level. If we tried to sit up our heads would bump the moist wooden roof. Each time I inhaled I could smell the rotting ceiling. However, I was in a location where I was able to see out the front door when they opened it. I could see what was coming. There were also two windows in the back that gave me the ability to see out the back. There was also a door in the back of the barrack that I hoped would remain opened during the day because there was a large bucket placed in the back of the barrack that was used as a toilet when we weren't allowed outside.

After we choose our bunks, the Blockova asked for volunteers to serve as kapos. Joli moved to join the others that were rushing forward. When I held her back she argued with me that being a kapo meant better food, clothes and a better chance for survival. All this was probably true but since I knew that we all couldn't be kapos, especially Goldie, I decided that it was better that we stayed together. I also feared that Joli, left without supervision, would get into trouble and end up in the gas chamber.

Joli continued to argue with me. I decided it was time to level with my younger sisters. They still did not fully understand or maybe they couldn't accept what had happened to Momma, Yidel, Mendel and Pearl. It was time to tell them what I had learned from the woman who had cut our hair and the man at the train.

"Joli," I said while holding her wrist, "you have to be quiet and listen."

Goldie had moved over and sat just behind us. She quietly said, "Joli's just trying to help. We do need food."

I looked at Goldie. Her face was streaked from dried tears. "I know we need food," I said.

Joli tried to pull herself free of my grip. "Let me go, please, Edita."

"Just listen," I pleaded. I must have seemed frantic because she stopped pulling and stilled. Goldie put her arm on my shoulder as if giving me permission to speak.

Then, abandoning all control, I blurted, "Momma's dead. She's dead and so are Yidel, Mendel and Pearl. They are all dead!"

"You can't know that, Edita!" Joli stammered in anger. Goldie began to cry.

"They were gassed. The woman who cut our hair told me, and I know that she wasn't lying. And, if we don't stick together we may be gassed, too."

Joli got so angry, "You're just saying this to keep me from volunteering."

I grabbed her and hugged her tightly, "I'm telling you the truth. Believe me, they're dead. I know it. The group of people lined up next to the first big building... that is a gas chamber... they were waiting to be killed."

Joli's glaring face was an inch from mine. I was preparing myself for her to unleash on me when suddenly she threw herself against the wooden bunk planks and screamed hysterically. I couldn't get her to stop. Goldie, was still crying, "I will die soon, Edita. I am not much older than Pearl...was."

A girl standing nearby overheard my remarks. I could hear her tell someone next to her that her brothers and sisters had been gassed. Girls started sharing their losses with each other and tears began to flow.

I repeated to Joli and Goldie that if we could stay together and we could survive. But neither could be consoled. Who could blame them, especially now that the truth could no longer be denied?

On the floor of the barracks, girls were fighting to be selected as kapos. I wondered what Momma would have had me do. I tried to usher up some of her good sense and wisdom, but nothing was coming to me. I could only repeat over and over again that I would take care of them. Momma believed that the strong should take care of the weak. That's why she went with the little ones. I finally appreciated what she had done for love. The beautiful lesson of her sacrifice was beginning to help me take on the role that she assigned me.

The sun was setting when the food came. The newly appointed kapos carried the food in metal containers to the bunks. It smelled like rotten potatoes. Each bunk was given a small pot containing a portion of the soup to be divided among ten of us. It came out to three swallows each. We also were given small portions of bread. My hunger was terrible but I gave two of my swallows to Goldie. We weren't given spoons so we sipped the soup from our single pot. Hungrily, we watched as each girl took her turn.

After "supper" we lined up and were marched to a specially built toilet room. The room was constructed like the shell of a barn. Inside was nothing more than three long rows of raised concrete slabs with holes in it. Each slab ran the length of the room. There were holes ran the length on both sides of the slab. We were all in terrible agony to relieve ourselves. We were corralled into the room. The girls at the front of the line quickly found a spot. Those in the rear had to wait or missed out on the using one of the holes. There was a lot of scrambling and pushing.

The kapos took advantage of the confusion to show force and mete out punishments. Much of the punishment was to please the Blockhova and SS and not to fulfill some sadistic desire.

"Hurry, Jews, we haven't got all night," the Blockhova yelled at the woman going to the bathroom.

The shouting, pushing and fighting for a spot created nothing short of a riot, which then in turn caused a waving of sticks to rain down on women in their act of defecating. The fear of the wooden wands and the risk of not finding a hole forced the women to relieve themselves on the ground where they stood. The odor and mess was sickening and caused some to vomit.

I managed to push through the crowd and found a place for us. I gave Goldie the opportunity to go to the bathroom first. I did my best to shield her from the sticks, hovering over her like a human shield. Joli went next. Finally, I had my turn. I had held my bladder and bowels for so long that I felt as though my intestines and bladder were being forced out of my body. It was painful, but a relief.

When we returned to the barracks, we found two blankets on each bunk. Ten of us huddled together, head to toe. The two thin blankets barely covered us but there was so much heat from our crammed bodies and the May weather that the blankets weren't needed. The three of us were scrunched against one another. I took the spot at the edge of the bunk placing Goldie between Joli and me. I was doing my best to keep the three of us snuggled together and safe.

This ended our first day in Auschwitz II- Birkenau.

***

Auschwitz and Auschwitz II-Birkenau are names that are ever imprinted in history as the embodiment of man's most extreme cruelty to man. It was the principal "Vernichtungslager," extermination camp, for the enemies of the Third Reich, particularly the Jews. Most certainly, if Hitler had triumphed in Europe, Auschwitz would have continued to exist as the killing center for all manners of nationalities held in contempt by the "Master Race." Millions of people were killed in the other death camps in Poland: Treblinka, Sobibor, Majdanek, Belzec, Chelmno.

It is not known how many hundreds of thousands died from shooting, hanging, pseudo-medical experiments, gassing, suffocation, starvation, beatings, torture, disease and exhaustion in camps designed originally as concentration camps, or as way stations to the death camps. The first of these camps was opened at Dachau, near Munich, on March 23, 1933, less than three months after Hitler's appointment as Reich Chancellor. Other such camps included Buchenwald, Bergen-Belsen, Ravensbruck, Flossenburg, Mauthausen, Gross-Rosen, Neuengamme, and Sachsenhausen. In all, there were, according to scholars of the Holocaust, approximately 400 detention, concentration, labor and extermination camps in areas controlled by the Nazis.

Auschwitz II- Birkenau was designated as the center for "special treatment," the Nazis' code word for extermination. It had its origins in early 1940. The site was a former military camp in the southwestern part of Poland, near the village of Oswiecim, some 30 miles from Krakow. By June 1940, the first prisoners had arrived. In total there were some 39 subsidiary smaller camps and facilities established in the Auschwitz environs.

By the fall of 1941, the main camp had a twin, Auschwitz II-Birkenau ("Birch Wood" in German) that had been built by war prisoners. Auschwitz III was later built. It was a complex of industrial works of I. G. Farben, referred to as Buna. They produced rubber products like tires.

Being in Lager C in Auschwitz II- Birkenau was a tightrope walk with fate. The typical stay in Lager C was so short that inmates didn't even bother to introduce themselves. Inmates were placed there as a supply chain for the gas chambers, medical experimentation and other such horrors. If trains arrived on schedule from occupied territories, inmates from Lager C continued to "survive"; if trains were delayed, inmates from Lager C made up the shortfall of the killing quota. During the spring and early summer of 1944, trains from Hungary arrived day and night as the Nazis headed toward their goal of being "Judenrein," free of Jews. From May 15 to July 8, 1944, some 430,000 Hungarian Jews were shipped to Auschwitz. The Nazis moved swiftly to exterminate as many Jews as they could before the Soviet armies could overrun Hungary, this made for some very smoky nights outside of Lager C.

CHAPTER FOURTEEN

ROLL CALL

THE DAY BEGAN AT 4:00 AM in Lager C. The kapos roused us by shouting and striking their clubs against the sides of the wooden planks of the bunks. It didn't take long for us to learn the routine. We would quickly jump down from our bunks immediately upon the wake-up call so we wouldn't be struck. We would bolt from the bunks and stampede through the block and into the night. Roll call, which was simply a head count, as we were prisoners without numbers, was conducted despite the weather.

"Rows of five," the kapos shouted while taking swats at both the laggards and the swift of foot. Everyone had to stand in line while we were counted. There was never an exception when it came to roll call. The sick were dragged or carried from their bunks, as were those who had died during the night. Corpses were laid out in the front of the first row, counted and then discarded.

In the darkness we stood. The searchlights cut across the sky, momentarily lighting up our shrinking shapes against the severe characterless walls of the barracks. There were times the searchlights would catch the crematoria chimneys spouting their pouring of smoke and I would think of my Grandma. I was so thankful that she died before this and was buried in her Tachrichim as she so desired. She may not have had a true headstone but at least we knew where she was buried. She didn't just blow away in the wind. Or worse, when the air was calm and dewy, the smoke would settle on the ground where we stood. The ashes of our fellow Jews gathering into a paste at our feet.

Typically, when roll call was completed and the numbers from the entire camp were reconciled, the guards released us from the hours of standing in formation. A loud dismissal whistle sounded. Those assigned to working squads and other duties would break formation and go to their assigned destinations inside the perimeter walls.

Those of us in Lager C were ordered to remain in place. The sun was well above the horizon and the day was getting hotter. Hairless as we were, the sun beat on our bare scalps, necks and faces. A girl of thirteen fainted and was dragged away by a kapo. I never saw her again.

We had been in formation since 4:00 a.m. without food or drink or a visit to the toilet. Many of the girls swayed from exhaustion, others shifted their weight from foot to foot. As time passed, more and more of the women could no longer contain themselves and dropped to the ground from exhaustion. Others could no longer hold their bladders and puddles of urine would pool between their feet. I was wracked with anxiety. *How can I help Joli, and especially Goldie? How were we going to survive?*

Suddenly there was a lot of commotion. I watched as the kapos became very nervous. Our formation was ordered to dress up its lines. I wondered what was going on. When I heard screams from the front, I risked stepping out of line to see what was happening. A thin woman was being selected and forced into a separate line; the kapos, clubs in hand, busily hustled the line of selectees into an orderly formation. Some of the woman in the selected group tried to get back into the main formation but were beaten for their efforts.

The selection committee moved closer to where we were standing. Among the committee were Dr. Joseph Mengele and Oberscharfurer Irma Grese. He was dressed in a striking Nazi uniform covered with decorations. He had a swagger to his walk that was recognizable. His presence demanded a compliance that he was receiving. His manner was cool, efficient and wordless as he cast his cold eyes along the line of prisoners. The SS moved swiftly into the ranks to drag out a girl or woman whom Mengele indicated by glance or nod. Mengele's practiced eyes stopped at the figures of the old, weak, small and very young. Having a noticeable nervous tick was cause enough to be pulled out of line. Instinctively we straightened our posture to appear healthy and strong. "Let me go, too," someone called out. Mengele granted her wish.

He was coming our way. I steeled myself for the moment of his approach as I tried to shield Goldie from his vision. It didn't work. Mengele grabbed Goldie by the arm and yanked her out of line. Goldie called to me. I forced back my tears and remained silent as Goldie was dragged to the new line of prisoners.

The long selection process was over. Our block was the last in the entire lager of 36,000 girls and women. This selection process was huge; our block alone accounted for at least some 200 prisoners. The final whistle sounded. We were ordered back to our block. The selected group was about to be marched off.

We had created a plan if Goldie was selected. Now, in the moment I hoped she could remember my instructions to her: "If you are selected, stay at the back of the group in the inside row. Keep looking for me, I'll come back for you, if I can." Goldie kept looking back at me and I kept my eyes on her.

Instead of following the orders to return to the block, I slipped along the fence and ran after Goldie's group being as careful as possible not to attract unwanted attention. When I caught up with the prisoners, the group was in a state of disorder, which was typical of selected groups, as girls would try run for it all the time. Kapos sallied into the lines with clubs swinging furiously and voices loudly cursing at the women and girls. The confusion and distraction would give me my chance. I dashed into the group and while the kapos were trying to control the other girls I pulled Goldie out of their clutches. When I first grabbed her arm, I pulled her towards the fence, she tried to resist, "Trust me," I said, out of breath. She knew she didn't have any other choice. When we got to the trench by the fence I pulled her down. We got away undetected.

"You came for me," she said, unsure whether to smile or cry.

"Of course I did," I told her.

We slithered our bodies along the trench until block 24 was in sight. We then stood up and carefully made our way to the block.

We reached the door at the rear of the barrack. This is where I had hoped to slip in but there was a kapo standing guard. I had no choice but to chance it. We were at bigger risk standing outside than trying our luck with the kapo. We approached the back door and the kapo, she seemed to understand what had happened. For whatever reason, instead of turning us in, she silently opened the locked door and let us enter. We arrived in time for our three swallows of soup. I wasn't sure why she just let us in however, this sort of luck, was going to be the norm for me.

We had hardly downed our tiny portion of soup when the kapos ran among us ordering us to get outside and line up again. We formed our ranks of five, but this time we were integrated with new arrivals to replace those who had just been selected for death.

We were in for another long spell of standing in the sun. After two hours, girls started to faint or fall to the ground delirious and sick. I stared straight ahead, the perspiration dripping down my face and stinging eyes. We were not allowed to help those who had fallen.

Tzatel, a robust girl from my hometown, fell to her knees and then over onto her back. I took a chance and looked over to see if she was alive or dead; her eyes were open. While no one was looking, Joli and I tried to get her to her feet. We knew that if she remained on the ground she would be hauled off and never be seen again. I slapped her face until I got her to respond. I could smell urine on her dress. We managed to get her on her feet.

"You need to stay on your feet," I whispered to her.

Tzatel stood in line with my sisters and me. Her eyes were closed and she swayed back in forth like a splintered tree in the wind, but at least she was upright.

We stood for several more hours waiting for the work squads to return. *Was the purpose of this exercise to further exhaust us and make us fit subjects for the selection?* There seemed to be no other reason for this treatment but sadistic cruelty. Even the kapos appeared to be wearied by the ordeal. They rarely roused themselves to punish those who whispered or got out of line by a few inches. But they were always on the lookout for their superiors. When the superiors appeared, they were galvanized into performing acts of authority and displays of zealotry. I don't know how Goldie withstood the torture; she was so small, yet so brave.

Darkness overtook Lager C. We had been standing almost the entire day, from sun-up to sundown. The searchlights had once again awoken to sweep their way across the camp. The air had begun to cool and I was beginning to get chilled from being soaked in sweat. The working camp outside Lager C was long dismissed but we were still standing in place. As I was to find out, this was to be norm on many days.

At last the kapos' shouts and a whistle announced that we were to be taken back to the block. "Supper" consisted of bread. I divided our share into five portions. Joli took two bites and her share was gone. I ate only half of my portion and then guarded the other half for Goldie's "breakfast." Tzatel only ate a little. She would survive the night but tomorrow would bring the same treatment and we would all be in worse shape.

The next night Tzatel said to me, "I am leaving this Hell by the next selection." And she did. I hoped that she had been selected for work. I never saw her again.

By the third day, I realized that my knowledge of so many languages was more valuable than the diamonds that some of the women had smuggled into the camp in their vaginas or rectums. A diamond could only be traded once, but my knowledge of languages proved useful many times over.

I learned about Lager C by listening to every conversation I could and questioning everything and everyone. I learned which selections were for death, which for work, and figured out what work details were safest if I were to volunteer. As soon as I could, I volunteered to bring the bread for our block; I didn't think that would be too difficult of a task. I quickly realized how wrong I was. For each delivery, I would have to stretch out my arms and hold them still while ten loaves of bread were piled on top of me. I had to balance all the loaves that were stacked above my eyes.

On my first day on the 'job,' I was waiting in line near the kitchen for the bread when I saw some carrots laying on the ground. As quickly as I could, I slipped out of line and picked them up. I hid them under my dress. Halfway back to Block 24, I was afraid that I would drop the bread because my hands went numb. I did not drop my load. The thought of fifty girls going hungry kept me going.

The next day my muscles were screaming at me but I volunteered again. The look on my sisters' faces when I handed them the carrots was worth it. I knew that I had to go again and try to scavenge to find whatever I could.

I had made them laugh with my comments: "Now you are my little horse, Goldie." I fed her like a pony, letting her bite the ends while I held the carrot over her head.

Keeping our spirits up was very important, finding reasons to laugh, extra nibbles of food, anything positive. That was what it was going to take to keep her alive. I knew what I was going to have to do at all costs and it was going to take more than volunteering. That night, when everyone was settled in, I snuck out of the barracks.

I was terrified. My heart was pounding. I was standing flat against the barrack wall. Those God-awful searchlights. I knew if I would crawl they would catch me. We often heard shots during the night, people crawling to steal food. I needed to be smarter. I had a dark dress that would blend in with the dirt and rocks. The searchlight wouldn't be able to illuminate my figure. The guards wouldn't be able to see my shape, or at least I hoped not. I sunk to the ground. I laid my body flat and began dragging myself in the dirt like a snake, I crawled in the ditch between the barracks and the fence to the kitchen. Whenever the searchlights passed overhead, I buried my face in the dirt. My heart was beating so loud. I was convinced that someone had to be able to hear it. It took me hours to make it to the kitchen but it was well worth it. The kitchen had just received a shipment of cabbage. When the kitchen help seemed busy, I grabbed a cabbage and dragged myself back to Block 24. I made it back inside and into my bunk unscathed. By the time I made it back, I thought my heart was going to explode from beating so hard during my foray and raid of the kitchen. I woke Joli and Goldie and showed them the cabbage.

"How?" she asked.

I put my finger to my lips to 'shush' her. She smiled and they took a leaf of the cabbage. I knew then that I would continue to take the risks – I would continue to fight to keep my sisters and myself alive.

CHAPTER FIFTEEN

THE MORE YOU KNOW

THE EARLY ARRIVALS TO AUSCHWITZ had been given most of the available jobs and had, at least for now, avoided the selection process. Some of these prisoners were assigned to work at the Kanada Building (where they sorted the belongings of the new arrivals.) There was plenty of job security there. The millions who arrived, and were being shipped into Auschwitz daily, brought with them small personal items: purses, suitcases, briefcases and the like. Jewelry, often heirlooms, gems and coins, were sewn into clothing. In Kanada, everything was separated into its appropriate pile: clothes, shoes, art objects, souvenirs, family photographs and money. All valuables and reusable items were destined for shipment to Germany, which by 1944 was in great need. These prisoners were treated a bit better than most and could steal bits of food that they found in luggage and clothing. There were others that worked in the kitchen, cleaning the toilets and even emptying the gas chambers.

About a week later, I ran into Sarah, a friend I had known in Mukacheve. She was one of the prisoners assigned to the Scheisskommando, the shit squad; this unit's job was to clean the toilets.

When we ran into each other, we hugged. I was happy to see her alive, for here, in this place, running into a friend or relative was a gift of life. She assured me that she was still my friend and that she would help me in any way she could. She was very upbeat in her speech, always pepping me up and telling me what was going on around the camps. This was how I had always remembered her but to see her smile here made me think that she may have just gone mad.

Sarah seemed to have a gift for intelligence gathering and interpreting whatever information came her way. It was a gift that would prove to be very valuable and I knew I found at least one person I could rely on. She had a very realistic view of things and she never let her energy level get zapped down by what she could not control.

"Where are you located?" Sarah asked.

"Lager C," I told her.

Sarah scrunched her nose. I already knew what she was going to say. I didn't want to make her say it.

"I have already heard it," I said.

Sarah looked down and shrugged but then told me that in spite of its reputation as being a camp without an exit -except through the chimney- Lager C sometimes sent prisoners outside the camp to work, even to Germany. But, she told me that the chance of getting into one of these rare and small transports was practically non-existent. Usually only the very strong were selected.

"Well, I am not particularly strong, and Goldie would never be selected for work so I am staying here," I said.

She was shocked that Goldie was still alive and gave me little hope that Goldie could avoid more than another one or two selections. In fact, Goldie could even be taken away between the formal selections. She advised me to do everything possible to get out of Lager C. She told me to take Joli with me, practically telling me to abandon Goldie to the inevitable fate of the very young.

"You can't take care of your sisters. It's a challenge to be able to take care of yourself. We are all living on borrowed time," Sara said. "Sometimes," she continued, "When Dr. Mengele is in a particularly sadistic mood, he will send all the members of a family to the gas chamber. He is well practiced in the art of picking out families, either by physical resemblances or by the way they look at each other or by how they stand in formation. How many selections do you think you can rescue Goldie from?"

My answer was simple, "As many as I can."

In my heart I knew that she was right. In theory, Auschwitz had no inmates under the age of fifteen. Goldie was eleven and had already cheated the exterminators several times. I was determined that she would continue to do so until the Russians freed us.

Sarah introduced me to one of her friends, Bayla, who worked on the Sonderkommando squad. This squad collected the corpses of those who had died the previous night in the crematoria and elsewhere. They performed the grisliest job of all but had a freedom denied to most of us, they could move about all sections of the camp. They could, at some risk, bring food and other items back to their barracks. Bayla was a wonderful source of information.

While Bayla was able to gather information around the entire camp, I was still able to do my part in my Lager with my extensive knowledge of languages. I realized that some of my best intel would come from the Russian prisoners of war that would were housed at working at Auschwitz II – Birkenau. Birkenau was also home to Italian, French and Polish POW's, all of whom had jobs at the camp and more freedom than the Jews.

One afternoon, while walking near the electric fence, I overheard two men speaking Russian as they replaced light bulbs atop the wooden fence posts that sat between barbed wire fencing.

"Can you tell me where Auschwitz is located?" I asked them in Russian.

The men stopped what they were doing and looked down at me from their ladders. "Why do you want to know?" the one man asked. "Are you planning an escape?" he asked with a chuckle.

"Don't make fun of me," I responded. "I just want to know what the nearest city to Auschwitz is, please."

"Krakow is about fifty kilometers away," said the other man, Niko, said. His face was kind and wrinkled with sadness.

The other man seemed to be enjoying my suffering, "Sorry. We don't have a map to show you. Don't worry; you'll never live to see Krakow."

"Who are you?" I asked.

"We're war prisoners from the Soviet Union. We have been here since 1941. We built these electric fences with the other Russian POW's. Most have all since perished. Some of us were kept alive to maintain the fences," Niko was matter-of-fact in his responses. I was inclined to believe him.

"Do you think the Soviet army is advancing our way?" I asked.

His answer was a patriotic one, "Our boys are fighters. They will crush the Nazis."

The other man added, "But they won't come soon enough to save you."

CHAPTER SIXTEEN

THE CZECH CAMP

T HE FAMILY CAMP WAS made up primarily of Jews from Czechoslovakia. It held thousands of prisoners brought to Birkenau from the Terezin ghetto. Families were housed together, including the children. There was no selection process immediately upon arrival and their personal belongings were not confiscated. Plus, the prisoners were allowed to send and receive letters and packages from the ghetto. The Czechs were under the protection of the International Red Cross whom had been monitoring them since the previous winter.

Before the war, we had family in Czechoslovakia who had maintained their Czechoslovakian citizenship. Every so often, I would venture to the fence and ask if anyone knew my cousin, "Rabbi Simon Rosenberg from Bratislava." Simon was the son of my father's sister.

One day, my cousin showed up at the fence, he had gotten word I had been inquiring about him. He had come just in time. I had heard from Bayla that the Red Cross was no longer going to be inspecting the Czech camp after the next visit. After that, the Germans were going to liquidate the camp. I told him what I knew.

"That is not true," he said. "We are under their jurisdiction. Your source is unreliable. God will take care of us."

"I do not believe there is a God here that gives a damn about us. Dr. Mengele is God in this place," I responded.

"Rifchu, you will see God will save us, you will see," Simon said.

* * *

A month later, a large group of Czechs were gathering near the fence. I raced over to see if I could find my cousin. He was there, hoping I would see the commotion and show up. He thought that maybe I had information on other family members. We were trying to talk but it was hard because the kapos kept chasing everyone away from the fence.

The kapos finally managed to clear the fence. Simon and I remained but at a distance which didn't seem to irritate the kapos. We were able to talk but needed to shout to get our message past the distance and the electrical, metal thrones.

"God saved us from the Egyptians and He will save us from the Nazis," he said.

"Save us? Are you kidding?" I scolded him with my questions, while implying that his head wasn't screwed on right.

"With God's help, the Russians will be here soon. If not, the Allies will come and put an end to the exterminations," he insisted.

My cousin being very religious and somewhat puritanical held a mystical view of God and saw Him in everything and everywhere. I could see that he had not changed in Auschwitz

although his beard had been shaven and his clothes were rag-
ged. Despite what had happened to him and Jews in general, he
was peculiarly thankful to God for saving some of His people. Of
course we were all glad to be among the survivors, but my cousin's thankfulness was from a serene acceptance of God's ways in
man's affairs, no matter how revolting the affairs turned out to
be.

I tried to make him see that God was not going to save any-
body, nor would the Russians, British or Americans.

"You need to pray more," he told me.

"Pray? We are praying to a false God. Look around Simon,
if this is what God let happen then God can go to hell, if there
is even a God," I shouted. I was spinning in circles. I was act-
ing crazy and cruel, transferring my own torments to a religious
man who had his own way of dealing with terror.

Simon stood peacefully watching me. He said nothing. I finally stopped. I stood still. My head dropped. I didn't apologize.
I couldn't. I had said what I meant. I calmly told Simon the information I had learned about the other members of our family.

While I was relaying the news, a young girl, around sixteen-
years-old, was talking with a woman who appeared to be her
Mother. I was so envious. I wanted my Momma so bad. My blood
boiled with jealousy as I watched the two of them together.

"Your two sisters had been among the early arrivals in Auschwitz. They had been tattooed and now were working not far
from the camp," I told Simon.

Bang! A shot rang out. The girl I was just so envious of was lying dead on the ground, the result of a bullet to the head. I heard
the Mother scream, as I jumped on jelly legs behind Barrack

twenty-two. The mother threw herself on the electric fence, her body shook until she was lifeless, omitting the smell of burning hair and flesh.

"See, cousin. Where is God now?" I asked, emerging from my hiding place.

I left my cousin frozen in his spot, his face filled with horror. I wondered later what this good Jew had made of the sadistic shooting and the subsequent suicide. I never saw my cousin again.

***

Weeks passed. There was a bustle of activity in the Czech Lager. The prisoners were cleaning up the camp: litter was picked up, the grass was tended to, and flowers were planted. During the time period the Czech camp did its cleanup work we were given post cards to send to our friends and neighbors. The instructions we received were that we could only write our names, the names of the family members that were with us, and a simple statement: "We are all fine." I wondered what the purpose of this exercise could possibly be seeing that most of our families, friends and neighbors were with us.

***

"Good afternoon, neighbor," the kind-faced electrician, Niko, said.

"What's so good about it," was my response. "Any news today?" I asked.

"Hang on if you can. My brothers are heading our way," he responded.

"No offense, but they are crawling in this direction. They are too slow for me, you too, I'm sure. What's going on around us? I've noticed that the Czech camp is cleaning up its surroundings. The garbage is gone by the fence?" I said.

"You mean you haven't heard? The Czech Lager will have special guests. All this preparation is in honor of the Red Cross who will visit in the next few weeks. I'm sure you received a post card to write about how good the Nazis are treating you?"

"Yeah?"

"A ruse for the Red Cross. Have a good day, and good luck neighbor," he said as he walked away.

On the day the Red Cross came, Lager C was not allowed to leave the barracks. We still had our head count, morning and night, but it was done in the barracks. SS women escorted the soup and bread volunteers. Nothing out of sorts could happen. It was pure propaganda for the Red Cross. Yet, the crematoriums continued to burn and the smoke continued to pollute the air with lost souls. *What did the visitors from the Red Cross make of the smell of the burning flesh? Why weren't they doing something about that?* If they really had a heart they wouldn't care about flowers and grass, they would care about the human beings next door that were being murdered. But so it goes.

After the Red Cross had their visit, the conditions in the Czech lager deteriorated rapidly. They must have had their rations drastically reduced because the people quickly became emaciated. Except for the family atmosphere, they apparently were not much better off than we were. For them too, diarrhea, dysentery, and other common debilitating illnesses ran rampant. As in our camp, two or three score died daily.

Early one morning, a couple weeks after my sad last visit with my cousin, the Nazis emptied out the Czech barracks. Hundreds of soldiers surrounded the Czech Lager and the inmates were ordered to assemble. They all knew what was coming and that there was no escape. They wailed and screamed, as they were force-loaded into the back of enclosed trucks. These trucks had been specially equipped with piping to direct the exhaust from the engines into the truck beds where the prisoners were packed.

The screams had muffled when everyone on the camp was loaded onto the trucks. The engines of the trucks began to roar. The Nazis revved the engines to hasten the asphyxiation. The muffled screaming and shaking of the trucks was lessened quickly. It didn't take long for the entire camp to be exterminated. Once the trucks were quiet, an SS Officer unplugged the tubing and the trucks drove the bodies to the crematoriums. The entire camp, thousands of people, were exterminated in a matter of minutes.

The SS were masters at assembly-line murder. Though the Czech camp was but a short distance from the gas chambers, they were smart enough to know that marching the thousands of Czechs to their death would have evoked chaos. This well thought out method was quick and efficient; in one day the entire Czech camp was reduced to ashes.

Every day, I learned more about Auschwitz II-Birkenau. In addition to the Czech camp, there was also a gypsy family camp nearby. It housed thousands of men, women and children. Niko had told me that the Nazis treated the gypsies better than the Jews because they were a wonderful source of "entertainment" for the Nazis. The gypsies received almost a sufficient amount of food and received medical attention when needed. They amused the Nazis with their seemingly wild music and dances. Like the Czechs, they were to survive until the Nazis had no further use for them.

The annihilation of the Gypsies occurred in August. They numbered in the thousands and were primarily Catholic. They owe their long stay in the 'Familienlager' (family camp) to Henrich Himmler who found them to be very a curious group. Himmler was the supreme head of the SS. He had a long-time fascination with the gypsies, considering them to be a mysterious race, a lost tribe perhaps descended from the Goths and Vandals. The Gypsies were held for study, thus they were allowed to follow their unconventional ways and traditions as they had always and to keep their possessions. Their only restriction was that they were confined. Because of the allowances made to them, they thrived. There were frequent visits by the SS to the Gypsy camp for the entertainment they provided.

When Himmler apparently lost interest in his gypsies, the entire camp was liquidated. The SS came in with guns and dogs, lined up the captives and told them they were being transferred to another camp. To reinforce the deception, the Gypsies were given bread and salami to take with them. Naturally, the Gypsies, having gotten used to favored treatment, fell for the ruse and reacted without fear and suspicion. The ruse worked beautifully. All night long the chimneys of the chambers belched and burrowed with smoke, dispersing the skin and bones of the ancient people.

CHAPTER SEVENTEEN

AND LIFE GOES ON

FROM WHERE WE STOOD IN formation, we could watch as the trains pulled into the station. Most of the trains arrived to Auschwitz early in the morning. The Nazis had well devised blue prints and plans to efficiently accommodate their process. As the fighting came closer, they expedited their killing, as though their very victory depended upon it. Dr. Mengele quickened the selections to help fill the gas chambers. A deep ditch was dug near the crematorium to help with the disposal of the bodies. My friends in the Sonderkommando estimated that up to 10,000 people died daily. The huge supply of human fodder was so great that the daily selections in Lager C were ignored.

The new supply of prisoners gave us a breather. Even though I felt cruelly selfish, I was relieved. Survival was the name of the game in Auschwitz, and I was determined that my sisters and I would survive.

Whenever I had the chance, I asked where the new arrivals were from. I knew many of the trains were coming in from Hungary and my Papa's sister and her family were from Budapest and my Momma's Mother and family were from Sholank. I was curious to see if they would make their way into the camp. I learned that my one cousin, Hannah, had arrived and was in another barrack and that my Grandmother, my Mother's Mom, had died in one of the female barracks in Auschwitz.

On one of my excursions to the kitchen, I snuck around to see if I could find Hannah. I had no luck. Joli and I then looked for her over the next few days. A couple weeks later, Joli found her in the toilets. It took lots of persuasion, but we finally convinced her to leave her barrack behind; we took her back to our block. She decided that she couldn't take the daily torment and decided she would take her chances volunteering for a work detail.

Often as I watched the lost souls marching to processing, I would relive my arrival in Auschwitz and Lager C. My mind, trying to protect me, only let me recall the memories in a jumbled fashion. My thoughts were not clear. I remembered begging my Momma to leave the children and come with me. I remember her telling me that she had to help the little ones die. *How could I have been so selfish? How could I have asked her to put Yidel down? Did little Mendel hear me ask my Momma to abandon him? Did he remember that I had promised to help him when he needed it?* The thoughts and memories haunted me. I kept telling myself that I had to stay alert and face the present – not the past. I had two sisters to take care of.

I often thought of my grandma, especially the times I noticed how much more weight I had lost. She would always order me to eat. I never was hungry at home. Grandma would always say, "Men like women with flesh on them!" How true. Even Dr. Mengele liked fleshy women. When the train shipments dropped to a trickle, he would do a selection of all the heavier woman and use their fat to make fuel, soap, or other pleasure for the soldiers.

We had been in Lager C almost three months. A lot of women and girls were gone. Some of the 'old timers' had survived because their family members were kapos and they had the benefit of extra food. The Blockova was good to them. I didn't have that benefit. Thus far, we were surviving on luck. I had been able to thwart Dr. Mengele's efforts to kill Goldie. I risked my life almost on a daily basis with my forays to the kitchen courtyard. I had heard stories of other women that had tried raids and been killed for their efforts, but I felt I had to continue this deadly game if I hoped to keep Goldie alive. Each day I prayed to my Momma for the arrival of the Russians. I knew that the chances were slim, but I had to at least hope.

In August, roll call became harder and harder to sustain. Even the climate cooperated with the Nazis. The sun burned through the clouds and scorched our exposed skin. The air was thick and weighed heavy in my lungs. The starving, malnourished bodies dropped like flies. The 4:00 a.m. roll calls started off with women fainting. The evening would end with death. Nights brought little respite from the misery. The women and girls would fight over a bit of bread. Finding a bunkmate dead was par for the course. The living would immediately seize whatever food or hidden items they found on the corpse. Groans, screams and crying had become the familiar sounds of the night.

It was awful to lie on the hard bunks packed with sweating bodies. We were packed so tightly that when one person turned over, all the bunkmates were forced to turn. It was normal to be kicked or to have an elbow smash into one's side or face. The stench of our filthy bodies and dresses never left us. Life was worsening by the day in Lager C.

Our most important task was to avoid daily selections, especially by Dr. Mengele and Oberscharfuhrer Irma Grese. To be selected was to fail to live out the day, even the hour. The challenge of selections was a game of chance and wit. Those that did survive can attest that it is impossible to explain why some lived and some died.

Once we tackled the first challenge of avoiding selection it was onto the second most important task: finding food. The rations that we were provided were designed to weaken and starve us to a slow and miserable death. I had heard that the anticipated life span, if you could escape selections, was no more than ten weeks: either from death by starvation or disease, whichever came first. Many of the women had resorted to eating the grass that had grown around Lager C. However, by August, all the grass had been devoured and all that was left was the baron earth. The only options were to steal or barter to get the necessary extras for survival. This became an activity known as organizing.

We had a term for those who failed at the second task; we called them Mussulmans, or walking skeletons. They had sunken eyes, sagging shoulders, and resignation written on their hollow faces. Most Mussulmans could not adjust to the dreadful conditions of the camp and were so paralyzed by their new environment that they withered away. They refused to, couldn't organize or parlay their talents and wits into getting something more than the camp offered. It was not uncommon for the most well educated people to be among the first to turn into Mussulmen. They simply could not cope with their new reality. It seemed as if their educated minds served them poorly. Auschwitz spat upon poetic, scholarly, idyllic or tender views of life. Not only were they special targets of the Nazis and kapos but fellow prisoners looked down on these people seeing them as impractical dreamers. Death followed them closely, usually in the form of the gas chamber. Rarely did a Mussulman overtly commit suicide; rather, they seemed to just lie down and die.

It was this subtle wish for death that one had to fight against constantly. Many times, especially when I was tired of fighting to keep myself and my sisters alive, I courted the idea of running into the electric fence or to trespass and get shot by a guard. There were even moments when I flirted with the hope that I would be selected for the gas chambers. These flirtatious thoughts of death rarely lasted long. My lust for life after all of this and the remembrance of my Momma's words energized me and helped me focus my resolve on finding ways to outlast Auschwitz.

One night Joli woke me and told me that in the morning she was going to volunteer for the next working squad assignment. According to her, nothing could be worse than our present condition. "I'll take my chances, so don't try to stop me," she said.

I tried to dissuade her with the claim that the Russians were on their way to free us, though in truth, I had no faith they would arrive any time soon. Joli took courage, but only after I made a desperate promise that if the Russians did not arrive in one week's time, I would not stand in her way.

Three weeks passed; Joli still wanted to get on the next selection but thus far I had been able to keep her with me. Many selections were made, yet the three of us were still alive. We watched as new inmates naively volunteered for seeming work details that were announced: nurse's aide, dressmaking, kitchen jobs, and other such phantom work and were never seen again.

Goldie was tired. She begged me to let her be selected and to save Joli and myself. "Take care of yourself and Joli," she screamed at me. "I am afraid that you will die with me and that was not what Momma wanted. They cannot kill us all!"

I knew in my heart that Goldie was right. My eleven-year-old sister was wiser than I. But I could not let go of her. She was my little sister. I had taken care of her all of her life. She was almost like my child. *How could I not try and save her from a cruel death?* I asked myself if I had done everything to keep up her faltering morale. *Was I being selfish by keeping her alive?* Joli's shouting broke my thoughts.

"Let her die! She is right. Then we can volunteer and save ourselves. It isn't fair that we should suffer for her!"

Without thinking, I turned away from Goldie and with all my force I smacked Joli across the face. I landed with such power that my hand stung. Joli quickly put her hands to her face and gasped.

"How dare you? Who do you think you are? I am going to protect her just as I am going to protect you. Don't you ever say such a thing again," I said, my hand throbbing.

Joli starred at me stunned. Truth be told, I was just as stunned as she was. Neither of us spoke for days. I wasn't sure how long the quiet would last but I knew I would have to do something to break the silence.

A few days later as I stood next to the block, I approached Bayla and asked if they would let Joli and I take their places for a day. I wanted Joli to see just what it was like inside the gas chambers and burning furnaces. I hoped that she would be so horrified that she would do whatever necessary to keep herself or Goldie from that fate. She agreed. I walked back into the block and tapped Joli on the shoulder.

"Joli?" I asked. She turned away from me. I got up in her face, "Joli, I was able to get you a job to try out for the day," I told her.

"Seriously?" she asked me, her head bobbed down, questioning my motives.

"Really. You and I are going to be Sonderkommando team," I answered.

Joli was excited and jumped down off the bunk. I told Goldie to stay hidden. I had dug a hole under the bottom bunk that she could fit in. I told her if it seemed like there were going to be any selections while I was gone to hide under the bed.

"We will be back soon," I told her, kissing her on the head.

I was completely unprepared to confront the huge number of bodies that were awaiting removal in all the blocks. Not all of the corpses had died of disease or malnutrition. Many were covered with bruises from beatings and other violent attacks. Our squad was not responsible for burning the bodies. It was our job to bring the bodies into the chamber. We did get close enough to witness the process. Those who worked the gas chambers were a very select group of male prisoners.

During their service, they were treated relatively well and could have as much food as they wanted, often choice pickings from the canned foods found on incoming trains. These men were the only ones permitted in the gas chambers and crematoria. They would remove the victims from the gas chambers and pile the corpses in front of the furnaces. They wore gas masks when they entered the execution chambers. They would have to pull the dead naked bodies off of each other. Because, apparently, as the gas rose toward the ceiling, terrible fights occurred as people struggled to get to unpolluted air, climbing on or trampling the weaker. Thus, many of the bodies removed from the gas chambers were covered with bruises and blood, their faces contorted in grotesque grimaces. They would then take the remains of the poor souls to the crematorium to turn them into smoke.

As we moved about the areas, I stopped to take a lasting look at the long of line of people waiting their turn to enter the gas chamber. Most of them stood so calmly in the line, unsure whether or not to believe that they were really going to be taken to a shower as the Nazis had told them. Then again, those in line didn't have a real understanding of where they were. All along the road there were posted signs that indicated that they were going to shower rooms, delousing stations, and distribution centers for new clothing. Those who knew that they were condemned approached the gas chambers with resignation, perhaps even relief. Most had been rounded up and treated badly in ghettos, suffered the deprivation of the long rides in sealed cattle cars, and had been set upon both verbally and physically. *What was left for them to live for?* That was the only comfort I could take as I continued on with my work.

We were told to pile the bodies across from the massive piles of clothing and shoes that been stripped of the dead before they were cremated. Even the gold fillings and teeth were extracted from their jaws prior to being turned to ashes. There were days that the Nazis gathered sixty-five to seventy pounds in a day of gold fillings a day. The gold was so voluminous that it became an important source of funds for the Nazi war machine.

Joli and I finished our day with the Sonderkommando just before the evening roll call. I could tell that it had given her just the jolt I had hoped for; it gave her a renewed determination to live and to help me in my fight to save Goldie.

In the months we were there, Lager C had seen its share of women and girls come and go. New faces arrived daily. No one who left the Block 24 ever returned. Goldie was now the youngest person in the Lager C. It was a miracle that she had escaped all the selections and the deprivation. There were days that I took the clay from the ground and smeared it on her cheeks to give her pale and sunken face a slightly healthier look so the SS wouldn't see her as sick at the time of selections. Goldie seemed to know that her days were numbered. We all witnessed selections that included girls that were older and stronger. There was no hiding the corpses lying on the bunks in our block or the smoke that was always in the air above. Yet, she rarely complained about her suffering. At night she would curl up and hug my waist and tell me that she loved me.

"I love you too, Goldie," I always responded.

"And you'll always be with me, Rifchu?" she asked.

"Yes, just like Momma always said, we're together, and that's what's important."

Her little hands squeezed me tighter. "I love you, Rifchu. Don't forget me, promise?" she said in a plaintive voice. In her sorrow she would always revert back to my given name, perhaps trying to remember a time when that was who I was.

"I promise. I will love you forever, no matter what happens." That was the only true promise I could make her.

CHAPTER EIGHTEEN

THE HOSPITAL

WE HAD SURVIVED SIX MONTHS in Auschwitz and we weren't doing too badly, all things considered. Part of me thought we had a possibility of pulling through. That was until one day I woke up to a leg full of tiny red blisters that quickly grew into large red boils.

From there, the color changed from red to purple to dark blue. Faint red lines like wispy spider webs began crawling up my side towards my stomach. The pain went from bearable to excruciating. I knew I had a fever. I feared the onset of gangrene in my foot. I was becoming more and more incapacitated by the day. I was certain the end was near.

I woke up one morning and my body was completely on fire. My head was throbbing and I shivered uncontrollably. I tried with all my might, but it was no use, I could not get up. I made Joli and Goldie go outside by themselves. I assured them I would see them later. A group of kapos gave me a once over, they too must have known that I was not long for this world. Without even a word, two of them picked me up and carried me outside. They tossed me on top of the group next to the corpses like I was already dead. In my head, I heard my Momma scream at me: "You must live; they can't kill us all!"

I was not going to fail my Momma! With every ounce of energy I had I crawled to the first line of five. I promised to give my share of rations to any one of them that would move to the rear and let me take their place in front. A woman quickly took my deal and I dragged my body into the woman's place, but I knew I could not stand, even if my life depended on it. As I sat in pain, a shout of "Achtung" made me look up. Oberscharfuhrer Irma Grese was standing in front of me. She wore a light blue shirt and white leather gloves under her uniform that was tailored tightly to show off her curvy figure. A gun holster sat low on her hips and held a silver pistol. She had sandy blonde hair, sparkling blue eyes and was no more than twenty-years-old. She was known as 'the beautiful beast.' It was rumored that she was Dr. Mengele's mistress.

I froze in fear. I was certain that she would pull her pistol and shoot me. I could not move. She pulled off her gloves and slapped my face with them. I was so weak that I fell over. She kicked me in the stomach; I doubled up in pain.

"Aufstehen, Jude," (Stand up, Jew) she shouted.

"I am sorry; I cannot stand up, SS Frau Grese. I am sick," I pleaded, still lying on the ground holding my stomach. I rolled over and pulled my dress up to show her the two huge boils and the red lines that were crawling up to my stomach.

She threw her hands up against her checks in horror and said, "Oh my dear God, you will die from that," Instead of shooting me, or pulling me out of line, she blew her whistle and called for the Blockhova, "She needs to go to the camp hospital right away. Tell Dr. Mengele that I am sending her," she told the Blockhova.

"Help the Blockhova take her to the hospital," she ordered the kapos.

I knew I had a fever, so it took me a moment to realize that I was not hallucinating. *Was she really worried I was going to die? Was she really helping me by sending me to the hospital?* Normally, a sick or impaired inmate was automatically consigned for extermination; SS Frau Grese was not known for gestures of pity. Joli and I had had run-ins with her before. On one of our many raids, Joli and I had made it out of our bunks to the kitchen and stolen cabbages. Frau Grese had caught us while we were sneaking back to our block. She made us kneel. When she asked Joli why she had taken a cabbage, Joli began to cry, begging her for forgiveness. Frau Grese hit her and kicked her in the chest. The beatings stopped only when Joli doubled over. Frau Grese then asked me the same question. I looked in her eyes and said, "I am sorry Oberscharfuhrer Grese. The cabbages were just sitting there and I am very hungry. I promise I will not do it again." She smacked me across the face with her gloves but unlike Joli, I did not cry and I did not show weakness and because of that I never received a beating.

But right now, I couldn't make any sense of what was going on. I wasn't even sure if I was happy going to the hospital or not. I had heard rumors about Dr. Mengele's hospital. They were only rumors because those that went into it never walked out alive. At this point, I had to take my chances, if I didn't go to the hospital, I would surely die.

The Blockhova and a kapo dragged me, one under each arm, my feet dragging behind me to the hospital block. When I got there, a Jewish nurse helped me to bed, there she washed me up with warm water and handed me a grey and white striped gown.

"What is going to happen to me?" I asked.

The nurse stayed silent, but tried to comfort me by taking my hand. She then escorted me to the next room. In this room was an operating table and a small instrument tray. The nurse told me to lie down on the operating table. She helped me up onto the table. I knew that fighting wasn't an option. I laid down. Fear was starting to set in. The nurse took my right hand and placed my thumb in my mouth and tied my hand around my head with a rope. She then tied my left leg and arm down. My heart started to race. I was trapped on the table. I had no way to escape. And even if I could find a way, I couldn't run.

As I lay there, I knew that if I was to survive this surgery I would still be killed afterwards. *Momma, did you make me struggle all this time just to suffer more and then die?* Tears started streaming down my face. Just when I thought I couldn't experience any more terror, Dr. Mengele entered the room and approached the operating table. I screamed out in fear but my thumb muffled my cries. He sat down in front of my foot like it was an inanimate object. He didn't acknowledge me or that my foot was attached to a human being.

"I need a minute-by-minute accounting of the time. Document, the time her eyes begin to roll back in her head, when they roll back and when she passes out completely. Understand?" Dr. Mengele asked the nurse, still staring at my foot. The nurse nodded. I looked at the nurse with pleading eyes but her eyes were now locked on her stopwatch. He picked up his scalpel. I knew now that this was really going to happen. I bore down with all my might. I expected pain, but when the scalpel made its first cut into my flesh I wished that I had died in my bunk. As the scalpel dug in and pulled through I felt like a fire was peeling the layers of my skin off.

I heard the nurse announce: "One minute. Two minutes."

Please, Momma. Help me die.

"Three minutes. Four. Five," the nurse continued to read off her watch.

I'm pretty sure I heard her say seven before I passed out.

I woke to a sharp pinch. It was a needle being stuck in my buttock. I heard the nurse tell Dr. Mengele that it appeared the medicine I was given was working. "She will make it," said Dr. Mengele said to the nurse. *What was he going to do now? Have me killed?* He unwrapped my bandage. Took a careful look just as if he was a real doctor. Dr. Mengele had saved my life.

The nurse returned to change my dressing. She was surprised to hear me address her in German. I asked her several questions about the surgery and my recovery. She told me that I had been asleep for three days and that I was expected to heal completely. I couldn't believe it. I was so relieved. I had survived.

"What will happen to me next?" I asked the nurse.

The nurse ignored me. The same women who had just answered several of my questions was now ignoring me.

"Do you know what will happen to me now? Will I go back to my barrack?" I asked her again.

The nurse continued to ignore me. I knew that wasn't a good sign. I had never met anyone that returned from the hospital. I needed to figure out a way to get back to my sisters.

All of the other women in the ward had undergone pain testing or some sort of experimental surgeries. I told the girl lying next to me that I wanted to leave the ward and go back to the barracks. She thought that it must have been the pain talking. She was happy to stay put in the hospital until the end of the war. Here, there were no roll calls, no selections, and the food was decent. She had also undergone surgery without painkillers yet she preferred the experience of the hospital to daily life in the camp.

On the other side of me was a girl who had undergone mouth surgery and could barely move her jaw. When I got close to her, she managed to tell me that every day her mother would come to the hospital and the kapos would chase her away. The next day when I heard her mother calling, I dragged myself out of bed and staggered to the back door.

"Do you know my daughter, Faygi? Is she alive?" the Mother asked through the crack in the door.

"Yes, she is alive," I told her.

"Oh, thank you God," the woman exclaimed.

I made a deal with her: I would keep her informed of her daughter's condition, if she would go to Block 24 and come back to me with news of Joli and Goldie. The woman happily agreed.

We were treated fairly well in the hospital. The nurses told us that we would be shipped out to work in the factories once we were well enough. While some of the girls believed this, I was certain that once our value to 'camp medicine' was over, our ends would be in the crematorium. But, in the meantime, I did enjoy the minor benefits of being in the hospital.

I didn't hear from the mother of the girl next to me for several days. I was worried that meant that my sisters had met a terrible fate without me. Finally, one night, the woman returned. I heard her hushed voice at the back door. The kapo was asleep in a chair at the end of the hall. I snuck out of bed and slithered on my belly towards the door.

She said that my sisters were doing the best they could but there was a new trigger-happy supervisor in Lager C. The lager was under stricter rules; brutality was increasing and, conditions were deteriorating even further, if that was possible. The mother was afraid that she would soon be selected to die and begged me to let her in so see her daughter. There was no way I could do that; we would both be killed if were caught.

Three days later, she returned again. The kapo was once again asleep in the chair. I dragged myself to the door. Before I could say anything, I felt myself being pulled out through the door and tossed onto the ground. When I turned around the mother was already inside the hospital, locking the door behind her. I was terrified to find myself outside the hospital in a hospital gown and barefoot. My only hope was to try and make it back to Block 24, without anyone seeing me. I knew that when I got there, the few friends I had would help me. I just had to get there.

I took to the small trench next to the barbwire fence. I laid down in the dirt and weeds as I had done on my many excursions to the kitchen. I slid on my belly the entire time. My head was fuzzy and throbbing but remarkably, I returned safely to Lager C and my block. I knocked quietly on the door. The kapo on guard let me inside. Luckily, she was half-asleep and didn't feel like bothering with me. Good fortune had certainly had been on my side the past several days.

I found my sisters. We had wonderful reunion, hugging and kissing. We chatted excitedly in hushed voices. Roll call was fast approaching and I needed to sleep; I kissed them both and told them I would tell them everything in the morning.

"One more thing, Edita," Joli said.

"Yes, Joli," I said my eyes starting to close.

"How are you going to go to roll call in a hospital gown?" she asked. Goldie gave me a look over.

"I am sure someone will die during the night. I will take their clothes," I said.

Joli was appalled, "You aren't going to make me undress a dead person, are you?"

My response was simple: "You will take me to the body and I will undress her. Now sleep," I said.

I was right on two counts. I had indeed made some friends, and someone did die during the night. When we heard one of our friends crying in the next bunk, Joli helped me to her side. Her sister had died. When I explained my plight, the surviving sister undressed the body and offered me her shoes and dress.

CHAPTER NINETEEN

DEEP IN HELL

A T THE END OF THE SUMMER in 1944, the German army began having its difficulties. The Russians were getting closer, and militia groups were fighting back. The gas chambers having pretty much completed the extermination of Czechoslovakians and Gypsies were ready to receive what was left of the Polish Jews, concentrated in various camps in Eastern Europe. The Polish newcomers were confined in an area between the barracks near the kitchen. We old-timers were sealed in our barracks. With the arrival of the newcomers our daily selections stopped. The Poles filled the quotas for the gas chambers.

During the time I had been in the hospital, Goldie's health took a turn for the worse. She seemed listless and had become even thinner. Her face was pale and she now wore a perpetual look of despair. It was harder and harder to keep up her spirits. I was determined I would start a new campaign to organize even more food; I was already aware of most methods. I understood the dangers of sneaking out of the block, day or night, risking the trigger-happy tower guards who enjoyed taking pot shots at the women looking for scraps of food among the garbage deposits. I was familiar with volunteering to carry the heavy loads of bread and soup, which were the least dangerous and usually the most fruitful way of getting extra food. As a volunteer, we could sometimes get near the great stores of food and snatch a potato or cabbage leaf. I often found a morsel of bread or food heedlessly discarded by one of the well-fed kitchen personnel. In my entire time in Lager C, I never saw a skinny kitchen worker. Instead of a bullet, those who stole food from the kitchen area would receive a good smack across the face or a blow from a stick. Because hauling food was so strenuous, many girls were too weak to do the work.

Having been a volunteer so often, I was a known face in the kitchen area. I even managed to make some friends and often found myself a recipient of their largesse. I would take the bread or whatever was given to me and place it in my dress. This was a bit of a problem because I had to make it appear as part of my breasts. Occasionally, when I was making my way to the block, I would be come upon other prisoners who would try to steal the food. I usually managed to escape, or I would let them beat me but I would never let them steal the food.

***

One night while I tried to sleep, I heard the sounds of the Mourners Kaddish, the prayer for the dead. It came from outside the block. I peered outside the back window, a large group of prisoners at the men's camp were being marched to death. They were naked and there was little left of them. They were hanging on each other for support. While some chanted their own Kaddish, others sang ghetto songs in Yiddish. They walked to their deaths bravely, none of them crying or trying to escape or fight their captors. Several of the girls in our bunk pushed open the back door so they could see what was going on outside. We all began reciting the Kaddish with them. It seemed that there was nothing else we could do.

***

Because life expectancy in Lager C typically short, we were not issued soap or disinfectants, nor were we allowed to have disinfecting baths that were occasionally allowed in other parts of Auschwitz. We were expendable, so it did not matter that our bodies became hosts to colonies of fleas and lice and the infectious diseases that ran rampant. Our clothes were never cleaned; therefore, they were a natural habitat for all manners of insects and germs. The barracks, including the blankets and wooden planks upon which we slept, teemed with vermin.

Efforts to combat these vile pests were impossible. All night long we slapped and scratched and picked at our crawling and jumping tormentors. Scratching the skin to get to the deeply embedded fleas and lice was a mistake, as vigorous scratching caused skin eruptions and open wounds that quickly became infected. Sleep only came from extreme exhaustion.

The infestation was so great that sometimes we often felt that we were being eaten alive. As the night cooled, and we huddled closer for warmth, insects invaded every part of our body, especially where our hair grew. It was common to see women groom one another like monkeys. Picking fleas and lice was an act of kindness, as futile as the efforts were. New arrivals, having had a brief disinfecting bath, didn't stay clean for long.

When summer ended and September began the weather

became cooler, especially during the morning and evening roll calls. Our thin dresses were utterly inadequate for the September wind and chill. Of course, we knew not to expect an issue of heavier clothing.

The cold weather was zapping our energy. As the weather grew colder, more and more girls were found dead in their bunks. If we thought the hot weather was bad, we were soon to find out it was nothing compared to the cold.

The death toll began to rise. People began to freeze to death and no one was surprised to wake up to an ice cold corpse in the morning. But a corpse meant a better chance for survival for someone else. The law of the jungle applied here. It was the survival of the fittest therefore, when I found a dead body, I would undress it and take her clothes so my sister and I could add another layer of clothes and bundle up. If I got lucky, there would be a morsel of food stuffed in the pocket. I can't say I was proud of what I had resorted to but I knew what I had to do.

Keeping up our hope for liberation served us well. I kept hearing that the Soviet army was pressing ever forward. News was that the Soviets had crossed into Poland and were pushing the Nazis back to Germany. Auschwitz, situated in western Poland, was in the direct route of the German retreat. We could hear the bombardments coming from the front.

As it turned out, the news was false. What seemed like a nearby battle was in fact a distant one and did not bring the Soviets any closer. My newfound friends in Lager C and I would sit and discuss why the Allies wouldn't come save us. *What were they waiting for?* To us, it seemed that they were hesitating so that the Nazis could finish us off.

All the while, the Nazis that were running the camp were be-having increasingly desperate. Despite that we had heard there was a shift in the war, the killing of the Jews continued. Fewer transports of Jews arrived each day. These new imports were arriving from other work or concentration camps. They were brought in for instant extermination.

Several huge pits were dug in honor of the prisoners who ar-rived in late September. These prisoners were marched direct-ly to the edge of the pits and shot with rapid fire. Their lifeless bodies tumbled into the pits. Those that survived the initial shooting tried to run. They were gunned down as they tried to escape. I no longer screamed or was even surprised when I saw such gruesomeness. I knew that I should have been. I mean, I was sad, as much for myself as for them. I had turned into some-one that could watch people being executed without unhinging. That is something the Nazis would have over me no matter if I survived or not. They would have forever changed me.

To get rid of the bodies, large fires were started in the pits. At times, the Nazis sometimes shot the Jews but didn't kill them; they let them fall into the pits to be burned alive. To keep the fires going, the Nazis didn't waste gasoline or kerosene, they fed the fires with fatter inmates. The flammable body fats ignited the skin and bones of the thinner bodies.

The fires raged day and night. The shrieks and wails of those waiting to die and those being burnt alive in the pits echoed about the autumn winds and drove the smoke and odor of the mass burnings for miles. But selfishly we were thankful for the warmth the fires brought. To be in Auschwitz II- Birkenau meant accepting the good with the most awful of tragedies.

Niko had told me that the pits were nearly fifty feet long and ten meters wide. He wasn't quite sure how deep they were but figured they must have been very deep because new victims were continually being added on top earlier ones. If they had finished burning all the new transports for the day the overflow corpses from the crematoria were burned in the pits.

During this time, the American planes flew above the camp, they were bombing some of the facilities near the Farban plants. If we could see them, we assumed they had to be able to see us. Even so, the trains continued to arrive. I wondered why the Allies didn't simply bomb the railroad lines. Surely the world was aware of what was going on in the death camps. *Why couldn't they simply drop a few bombs on the rail facilities, the gas chambers and the crematoria?* Such bombings would have saved a lot of lives by slowing down the killings and burnings. Some of us would have died in these raids but at least it would have been for a good cause.

CHAPTER TWENTY

BLOOD DRAIN

I T WAS THE DAY OF ATONEMENT: Yom Kippur, 1944. We were confined to the barracks under special guard.

"Achtung!" screamed the Blockova. At her command we stood at attention, the order seeming more insistent than usual. In marched a delegation of SS along with SS-Oberscharfhrerin Irma Grese, and Hauptstrumfuhrer SS Fritz. I had never before seen such a large a group of high-ranking SS. Something was going on.

Oberscharfhrerin Grese called the Blockovas for a private conference. She had visited the barracks on other occasions but never with such a delegation in tow. The Blockova called for her assistants and the muted conference continued. The meeting ended and SS Grese slowly walked down the length of the barrack, stopping now and then to peer into a bunk, her escorts following behind her. Finishing her inspection, she engaged in another conversation with the Blockova. As quickly as they came, SS Fritz, SS Grese and their entourage, left.

The kapos called out for us to remain quiet because the Blockova had good news for us. She told us that the Haupt-

strumfuhrer had ordered a double ration of bread in the celebration of Yom Kippur. Therefore, she needed fifty strong girls
to go for the food. The news of the double ration of bread elated
most of the girls in the barrack. But, my sisters and I did not join
in the celebration. We strongly distrusted proffered gifts, especially from the SS.

I was very concerned. I had heard from a Russian prisoner
that selections would be made in the near future, selections for
blood draws. I knew from previous selections that the Germans
preferred the blood of blond, blue-eyed prisoners. Given that
Joli and I were both blond and blue-eyed, we had devised an
escape plan to avoid any selections. I knew that it was going to
be time to put our plan into effect.

Goldie looked anxious so I took her in my arms and held her.
I asked her what was on her mind.

"Why do you look at me like that, Goldie?

"You no longer believe in God, do you Edita?"

"Do you?" I asked.

"I think so. I think Momma would want me to," Goldie said.

"I'm glad you believe in him. I'm sure Momma would want
you to, just as she did all of her life," I said, avoiding the question.

I gave Goldie a big hug and promised her that we would be
back when it seemed safe. Joli and I kissed her and we jumped
off the bunk to put our plan into effect. Joli approached the kapo
guarding the rear door. As Joli got close, I gave her a hard push
so that her body knocked the kapo down. I ran and opened the
door of the barrack. I grabbed Joli and pushed her out ahead
of me. Before I could get out the door, the kapo sprung to her
feet and grabbed me, shouting for help. I couldn't free myself;

the kapo was much stronger than I. The kapo, using her stick, pushed me back into the barrack. I went flying against the side of a bunk.

Not wanting to attract further attention, yet being trapped inside the barrack, I slid under the lowest bunk. I could hear that the Blockova arrived to collect her selected girls. She shouted orders to the frightened kapos.

"You over there, I want only strong girls. Now get this lot lined up facing the rear door," she ordered. The kapos hurried to obey. From where I lay I could see the feet and ankles of the girls. Then the Blockova's fancy shoes came into view. Realizing she didn't have 50 girls, the Blockova ordered a girl named Pola to get off her bunk and join the selectees.

Pola cried out, "I am sorry. I cannot go today. I am sick. I promise to go tomorrow."

The Blockova would have none of Pola's excuses and gave her a swat with a stick. Pola's cousin was a kapo, but pleading was of no use. Pola was forced to join the selectees but not before she received several more blows from the Blockova's stick. Apparently the Blockova was satisfied with the chosen group and turned to march them off. Suddenly, Pola, with the help of her sister, managed to break away from the group, she ran down the kapo guarding the door, and escaped outside.

"Where is your sister?" the Blockova shouted.

"Perhaps she is hiding under the bunk," Pola's sister replied pointing at me.

That is how I got caught. I was called out by another prisoner. I couldn't blame her. That was how it worked here. You protect yourself and your family above anything else. The Blockova went wild with anger. She kneeled on the floor and beat me with her stick. I couldn't escape, no matter how small I tried to make myself. I did the only thing I could think of: create a panic.

I started shouting, "The Blockova is making selections for blood! Our bodies will be fully drained of blood for the German troops at the front!"

When the girls in the block heard this they began to shout, scream and scramble about. I could hear Goldie pleading for my life. All I did was make the "Blockhova" (make a decision on the spelling of this word, as you sometimes you write it without the "h") very angry. The wooden planks of the bottom bunk were lifted and I was hauled out of my hiding place like an animal from its lair.

"You'll pay for this!" she screamed. She was out of breath but was still beating down on my shoulders.

I kept screaming at her and struggling to get away from the kapos but they held me down. I was well beyond controlling my fury. I lashed kicking, screaming and thrashing about. I screamed at the Blockova, "You Nazi collaborating Bitch! You get fancy dresses and scarves for your hair. You have fancy food and are well fed while we freeze and starve! Now, you want fifty girls to pay with their last drop of blood so you can keep being well treated by the Nazis? I will not die giving my blood to the enemy. If it's such a good thing to give blood to the Nazis, send them your Mother. She is bigger than most of us. She'll give them more blood!"

I saw her face go white. She was fuming. Her eyes bugged out, her red mouth was contorted to one side and her body shook. She was stunned at me for calling her a collaborator.

"You filthy bitch! I've suffered too these past four years. How dare you accuse me of being a collaborator? I'm trying to survive just like you are," she screamed.

I was not to be controlled. "We are going to pay for your suffering and safety?" I screamed back. I saw her stick heading for my head; I hoped she would kill me with the blow. "You'll pay for this!" she ranted. More blows rained on the left side of my body. I felt faint and was close to being unconscious when the beating stopped.

Goldie called my name but her voice sounded so far away. Someone helped me stand up but I was still too delirious to see if it was friend or foe. They left me wobbling in place. My blood felt sticky and warm as it flowed down my face. I was wobbly from the beating but I was up. The back door was opened and we were ordered to march to our destination in a different block. My faculties had returned but my body, especially my arms and stomach ached. The early signs of bruises were starting to form from the beating.

I was going to follow Momma's rule of never being first so as I approached the entrance to the new block, I managed to work my way to the end of the line. The line slithered forward slowly. At the front of the line was a woman, needle in hand, pricking each girl's ear and testing a small amount of their blood. The girls who 'passed' the blood test were pushed through into another line to be processed.

In a large pile in a corner at the far end of the large room was a pile of bodies. These corpses were a chalky white; very different than the other bodies I was used to seeing.

Oversized chairs lined the right side of the room; a nurse

waited in attendance behind each one. White refrigerators were on the left side of the room. A large pile of chalky white corpses were piled in the far corner of the room, their limbs tangled like broken kindling waiting to be burned. Dr. Mengele stood behind the live patients who had passed and two other doctors were disposing of the failed patients.

The girls who had failed the tests were disposed of by a lethal injection of kerosene. These girls would begin shaking uncontrollably as soon as the liquid hit the vein, and then as quickly as the shaking began it would stop and they would fall flat. Some were still shaking when they were thrown on the pile of dead bodies. No one walked out alive. This way the Nazis' secret was safe.

I moved forward; I had figured out how the process worked. Three girls escorted to the chairs at a time. They were securely strapped to the chairs, needles inserted into their arms. Large vials were attached to the needles and the vials filled rapidly. When the first vials were filled, a nurse would hand Dr. Mengele fresh ones. One of the girls tried to speak, but a hand was clamped over her mouth. She tried to struggle, but she was too weak, she closed her eyes. Another vial or two of remaining blood was drawn; the girl died and the needle was pulled out. Her corpse was dragged away and her body joined the others on the pile. A new girl was brought in to replace her. The process was repeated over and over. I heard Dr. Mengele's say, "Good," replying to a nurse who reported how much blood had been drawn.

The line moved forward. The girls in front of me were frightened but knew they were trapped. The guards moved closer to them, flourishing their clubs in hopes of quieting them down.

There seemed to be no way to escape. If anyone broke ranks, they would be clubbed and their blood would be drawn anyway. *I'm sorry Momma. I've reached the end of the line. Why did you make me go with Goldie and Joli? Who will take care of them now?*

I thought I heard my Momma scream, *"They can't kill us all!"* Or maybe I screamed the words; at that moment I couldn't have been sure.

My blood 'passed' the ear test. There were only six girls left. A guard shoved three girls forward with his rifle butt. In my head I heard my Momma scream, *"There is always time to die. You can't help them. Save yourself."*

The guard seated the last two girls and me. Dr. Mengele dismissed the SS guards and the kapos. He began administering the needle into the arms of one of the girls. I watched as the SS guards and kapos left the room. Now, without any guards in the room, maybe, I would have a chance.

A nurse took my arm and pushed me into the chair, "Don't be afraid. It won't hurt. It is like falling asleep," she said.

She removed her hand from my arm to get the straps. The warm blood from the previous girl began soaking through my clothes. *Was I to end up a bloodless corpse? Not while I had an ounce of blood in me to prevent it.* They were going to have to fight me for my blood.

"You can't kill me!" I shrieked. I bolted up from the chair, leaving the straps dangling in the nurses hands.

"Stop! Sit down!" Dr. Mengele shouted at me.

I ran as fast as I could towards the door, knocking over trays and pushing through the nurse. Dr. Mengele and the nurses had no choice but to remain where they were to control the other two girls. Dr. Mengele began yelling for the guards but I was already out the door. I was running as fast as I could. My lungs felt like they were going to explode. I knew that the kapos had to be pursuing me.

I ran toward a group of new arrivals and sunk down between them hoping the kapos would lose me in the group. One of the girls began yelling at me, "Get away from us. You will get us killed. She is here." I wasn't sure why she thought I was going to get her killed, she was already in line for the gas chamber. But, they didn't know any better; they probably thought they were in line for the showers.

"You are in line for the gas chamber," I yelled, hoping that the chaos it would cause would help cause a diversion as I kept running. The group began to panic. The once still line was no fluttering like a swarm of angry wasps.

I could see the kapos in front of one of the blocks. I darted away from the buzzing women and ran around another building. I was in a manic state, my heart was racing faster than it had ever before, my head began to spin. I had no idea what to do.

Where to hide? I saw an SS guard and heard him scream for me to stop. I heard a gunshot but did not feel anything. I would have welcomed a bullet if it would keep me from Dr. Mengele. I was running out of space and was trapped between the electric fence, the guards and kapos. I zigged and zagged until I found myself near the latrine. The Scheisskommando were at work. I ran among them. Someone grabbed my arm. *My heart stopped, had I been caught?* It was Sarah.

"Can you hide me? They want to kill me," I puffed out the words. She pulled me toward the rear of the latrine. I could hear the shouts of my pursuers outside. They weren't too anxious to enter the filthy building. My friend, my savior, pushed me behind a brick stove and covered me with a dirty towel. She was brave to do this, for if caught, she surely would have been shot on the spot.

"Where is the girl who ran this way?" one of the SS demanded.

"Who?' Sarah asked in a voice that suggested that the questioner was a little crazy. "Oh," she said, "You mean that nut! She ran through here and out the back door." My friend was apparently very convincing because the SS quickly ran out of the toilet room, the kapos at his heels.

The barking of a pack of kapos woke me, "Here she is!" I wasn't sure how long I was sleeping in my hiding place, but I could tell the sun must have set.

A kapo stood over me, "Get up you stupid bitch, the whole camp has been looking for you for over three hours."

I tried to stand but my legs were stiff. They pulled me up but I could only stand by holding onto the stove for support. My stomach ached and my legs were lifeless. I asked them to help me but my voice was only a whisper. One of the kapos pronounced me crazy, "How did you get blood all over your dress?" The sirens were wailing throughout the camp, someone had escaped, presumably me.

"Please don't turn me over Dr. Mengele," I pleaded. From the looks on their face I could see they were puzzled. I then realized these kapos didn't know what I had fled from or why I was hiding.

My legs were numb from being crunched in my spot and I was unable to walk so the kapos dragged me out of the latrine. It was dark outside; I had no idea how long I had been hiding. The chilly air was bracing. I began to recover. Block 24 was visible, but I feared telling the kapos that it was where I belonged. I was afraid that the Blockova would turn me over to the SS and that she would also turn Goldie and Joli over to them.

The kapos brought me to Block 18. Apparently, Block 18 had a girl that had been missing for over three hours, I took her place. Someone else had taken my place in Block 24. This happened at times. Because of the constant coming and going of prisoners, it was difficult for camp supervisors to keep track of individuals. All they cared about was that the numbers matched their records.

The girls in Block 18 were less than receptive to my being there. They wanted to know why I smelled like the latrine and why I was covered in blood. They called me terrible names and ordered me to leave. I pleaded with them to let me stay until roll call was completed. I offered them my ration of bread not to kick me out or tell the Blockhova. They agreed.

I sat in the back Block 18 my knees pulled up to my chin feeling deserted and alone. I was doing all I could to hold back my tears. In that moment, I didn't care whether I lived or died, I just didn't want anyone to kill me.

That night I left Block 18. As I made my way back to Block 24, the electric fence was calling to me. Its' wires glistened from the searchlights overhead. The webbed coils were right there; I thought I would run toward it; embrace it. There may be a moment pain but it would be exquisite compared to the pain of my present life. In a few minutes my body would stop dancing on the wires and I would be free of Auschwitz, free of my miserable existence.

Yes, yes, that's what I would do. And I hoped that Momma would understand and forgive me.

It was but a short run to the wires. I crouched, ready to spring. But my legs would not move. My feet were frozen to the ground. Momma's face flashed before me. She screamed at me to take care of my sisters *"Return to Joli and Goldie. It is not your time to die, there will always be time for that,"* she said.

Tears rolled down my face.

CHAPTER TWENTY-ONE

CLEAN-UP

THE KAPO GUARDING THE REAR DOOR of Block 24 was asleep. I slipped past her and made my way back to my bunk. The barrack was terribly cold and a draft roared down the aisle that separated the line of bunks. It was colder inside than it was outside. I tried to block out the moans and groans of the suffering of the restless sleepers. But, I couldn't block out the familiar sobs of little Goldie. I rushed towards the sound.

"Rifchu, we thought for sure that you were dead, that this time you couldn't get away," Goldie said, tears pouring from her blue eyes.

I crawled in beside her and held her tightly. Her body was quivering from the cold. I hugged her tighter. In that moment I was reminded why I was kept alive.

"I told you I wouldn't leave you," I said as I curled up next to her. It didn't take long for me to fall asleep.

Morning came quickly. I knew the first thing I had to do was change my blood soaked dress. It wasn't going to be a hard task. When I climbed down from the bunk I stepped on a girl below that had died during the night. I took off her dress and layered it over mine. One bunk down from us was a girl dying of scarlet fever, she was gasping for air. Her sisters sat near her side. The sick girl begged them to let her be gassed and to save themselves. I held Goldie's little hand tightly and kissed her head. I never thought I would be so happy to be walking out to roll call with my sisters.

Goldie stood between Joli and me. Her eyes said that she was ready to give up and die. I understood her desire all too well but I was not about to let that happen. I held tightly onto her little frail hand.

The sisters of the sick girl fell in line next to us. They had left their sister behind for collection by the Sonderkommando. Perhaps, if she were lucky, she would be dead before the Sonder-kommando arrived.

"It was cruel for the sisters to leave the girl behind to die alone," Joli whispered.

"If it comes to it, we will die together," I whispered back, glad that Joli was showing solidarity to our family unit.

The Blockova made her way up and down the line counting head after head. When she saw me she stopped. I stood tall, I showed know fear. She leaned forward, her nose but a few inches from my face, "The next time you cause any trouble you will be sent right to the gas chamber, do you understand?"

"Yes, Blockhova."

She did an about face and continued counting. The vengeance in the Blockova had escalated since we had first arrived. I wondered if she was going half mad from the stress or if part of her had always been evil. She had no reason to send inmates to the gas chamber for reasons other than volunteer work but it seemed she was starting to enjoy her work.

When her counting was done, the Blockova sounded her whistle and called for, "volunteers for factory work." It was more than likely that everyone was volunteering for death, but even so, people kept stepping forward.

It was so cold outside. We were shivering, rubbing our arms, and stamping our feet, bouncing around, anything we could think of to keep warm. We were relieved when selections were over, hoping we would be able to go back to the bunk so we could snuggle close to try to keep warm. When we weren't released we began to get restless waiting for an order, and then it came.

"Strip!" The Blockova ordered.

The ludicrous order was received without response. Did they really expect us to strip in the freezing cold? When no one moved, the kapos moved among us with their sticks smacking our legs and arms shouting, "Strip! Strip!"

We tore off our thin, foul dresses but kept on our shoes as ordered. We stood in place, naked and shivering for over an hour until we were finally told that we were going to be given a delousing spray and a new dress.

I was terrified for Goldie, unsure if there were selections before the spray. Joli and I did our best to sandwich her between us in an attempt to keep her warm and hidden.

To our surprise, we were each even given a thin blanket as we were marched out of the gates of Lager C. A group of inmates played music for us as we left the Gates of Lager C. It was peculiar to say the least. As we marched, we were told that we were being taken for processing. I had no idea what that meant but we were heading to the original portion of Auschwitz, away from Birkenau, which seemed like a good thing because it was away from the gas chambers and crematoria.

We stopped at the same place that we were given a shower and shaved on the first day we had arrived at Auschwitz. We were to wait our turn to be deloused at the Kanada. Several groups of prisoners were being hustled from place to place. There was a sort of organized chaos ensuing. SS guards and their dogs were posted at several locations to ensure that there was no mingling or mixing of groups. Each time a new group approached, we were pushed back to make way.

In one of the passing groups I recognized a cousin who had lived near us. When she saw me she forgot herself and jumped out of line to hug me. Within a moment a German Sheppard growled and strained its master's leash. My cousin quickly jumped back into line. We never got to embrace and we never saw each other again.

We moved closer to the tables and the men that were going to shear the hair from our bodies. Each girl was given the order to lie down on the table and to spread their legs. The men quickly scraped the straight razors across their skin removing their pubic and underarm hair. Following the shaving, their bodies were sprayed with a disinfectant.

We neared the table. I held my shoes in front of myself to cover what I could. A young SS officer ordered me to stand at attention with my hands at my sides. "Do you think I want to see a Jew's vagina? I am sick of looking at you pigs," he sneered in disgust.

I dropped my hands and my head. I was given a shove towards a table. Two men held my legs while a third scraped away.

I felt the dull blade pull and cut. My legs were pulled further apart to get at the hair that was lower down. I wanted to cry out in humiliation. I'm sure the others did, too. I clenched my teeth so as to not make a sound. I knew that the sneering SS officers were staring straight at me and I was not going to give them the satisfaction of crying.

I was given a large spray of disinfectant. The SS shot the spray straight up me. It felt like a small fire had been lit inside me. The alcohol also burned in all the places that the razor had torn through my skin. But I did not show pain or fear. I slid of the table feeling a little triumphant, they did not see me cry.

What followed next was an ice cold shower. I hadn't had a shower in over six months. It felt so good to have the grit and grime slide off of my body. As cold and prickly as the water was, I was grateful for the frigid shower. And even though the soap we were given to use had been made of the body fats of Jews burned in the ovens or pits I was glad to have soap.

When we finished showering, we were not given a towel. We tried to squidgy ourselves with our hands but were left to air dry in the frigid temperatures. Despite the shower our bodies still reeked of disinfectant and the smell was overwhelming as we made our way back to the room to get new clothing.

There were tables of clothes. SS guards told us to take an article of clothing and stand in line. I managed to get a warm dress for Goldie. It was much too large and dragged on the floor. I tore of a piece of the dress and fashioned a belt so that it held snuggly against her body. Joli's dress was rather thin and large on her, as was mine but we felt rather fortunate because our outfits were clean and not torn or shredded as our discards.

We were marched back to Block 24. The smell of disinfectant overtook the barrack. It was so strong but at least the stringent smell kept the lice off our bodies. We were all ready for a night of undisturbed sleep.

How easy it was to be lulled into a false sense of security. *If they were going to kill us, why clean us up first?* But we were quickly to revert to our normal Lager C state of terror and wariness.

CHAPTER TWENTY-TWO

ONLY THE GOOD

THE CROWNING ACHIEVEMENT OF SS-Obersturmbann-
fuhrer Adolph Eichmann's diabolical career was the
deportation of the Jews of Hungary to the death camps.
Hungary was the last country in Europe where there was a very
large concentration of Jews, some 850,000. It has been rumored
that in March 1944, in Budapest, Eichmann asked the assembled
Jewish Council of Hungary, *"Do you know who I am?"* He then
answered his own question, *"I am a bloodhound."*

Eichmann was scavenging Hungary and elsewhere sniffing
out any of the remaining Jews. No one would escape his net, not
if he could help it. Those who dealt with him in Hungary, especially in late spring and summer of 1944, reported that he was
frantic and voracious about finding and discarding the Jews.

Though the German army was being pressed on all fronts and
the war was all but lost, the Nazis still fought with the tenacity of
pit bulls. In the West, the Allies were completing the recapture
of France. In the East, the Russians, already in Poland, were entering Hungary and advancing westward. *But would they arrive
in time to save the remaining prisoners in Auschwitz?*

The long-time residents of Auschwitz and Lager C had grown skilled at the art of thievery and bribery necessary to stay alive. The girls had learned that they had one tradable good that could be traded over and over and there were always plenty of SS Officers and Prisoners of War who had many privileges, extra food, and goods that they were willing to trade for sex.

It was a common occurrence to find girls in the back of the barrack with the POW's or soldiers trading sex for a coat or food. We just ignored the acts and never spoke about them. I couldn't blame the girls who chose to sell themselves. We were all desperate to survive. However, that wasn't an option for me, and I would not let that be an option for my sisters. Part of survival was keeping our pride, just as Momma would want us to. Plus, engaging in that type of behavior meant putting yourself in risk of diseases and pregnancy. One girl who did get pregnant ended up in the hands of Dr. Mengele and that was the last place anyone should ever want to be.

It was a cold fall day but even so I needed air and I needed to be alone. I told Joli and Goldie that I was going to sit outside and I would be back later. There was a spot outside the back of the barrack that I found where no one would bother me. It was a place that, despite being surrounded by thousands, I could be alone. I sat down, tucked my knees to my chest and tipped my head to the sky. When the wind blew it would bite my exposed skin but I did my best to ignore it. I hoped that if I could make myself light enough the wind could just take me up, up and away. But, I remained on the grounds of hell. So, I went back into the devil's gut.

When I walked in I could see Goldie sleeping in the bunk but I couldn't find Joli. I looked around and started asking the girls in the bunks, most of who replied with uncaring shrugs. Finally, one of the girls pointed to the back of the barrack. All I could see was a POW holding up a coat. I tried to peek around the prisoner but I couldn't see past him. My blood started boiling. *Was Joli really going to sell herself for a jacket?* I stormed forward and threw the POW off of the girl and it was indeed Joli.

"Get the hell off of my sister!" I screamed at the POW. He just stood there. "Get the hell out of here!" I yelled again. He had dropped his jacket. I picked it up and threw it at him. "Go!" I said shoving him.

"Stupid bitch. Freeze to death!" He said, leaving.

I was so angry that I smacked Joli across the face, "How dare you?! I try to protect you and you do this?"

Joli tried to run at me, she had over two inches on me and a good twenty pounds but my anger gave me strength. I pushed her back, "Don't you dare touch me, Joli. It is because of me you are alive right now. I will continue to do that but don't you do something so stupid again!"

Goldie had woken up to catch the end of our fight. Her face was sad. I climbed up on the bunk and laid down next to her.

The next day I went out and found my Russian POW friend, Niko. I asked him if he would be able to get me a jacket. I told him that I had nothing to trade but my appreciation. His sad old face smiled, "That is enough," he said. The next day he gave me a jacket he got from the Kanada.

I brought Joli the jacket, "But how?" she asked.

"Just don't ever let me catch you in the back of the barrack again," I told her.

We never spoke of her actions or our fight again.

***

In early October, a different type of prisoner arrived in Lager C. They had a long familiarity with the brutalities of the Nazi overlords. They had endured years of terrible treatment in slave labor camps, factories or ghettos. They had battle-hardened experience that would serve them well here. These girls and women were aggressive and vicious to the extreme. They did not need a period of acclimation to the camp to learn what would keep them from the selections, the beatings, and from starvation. They had no tears to shed and they feared no one. They also knew how to prey on the other prisoners.

During their first night in Lager C, I learned firsthand of their ruthlessness. Four girls and I were carrying a large iron cask of soup from the camp kitchen when eight of the new arrivals snuck up on us. They pounced on us, fists flying, knocking us to the ground. With the soup in their possession, they pulled off their wooden sabots (shoes) and used them as ladles. We protested, I most vociferously. They mocked me when I complained about their cruelty and their selfishness in depriving all the other girls of their meal. I was called naïve and stupid. They told me that the good die first and they were not ready to die. All of us in the Block 24 went hungry that night.

As it happened, the next day I had the opportunity to talk to one of the new girls. She told me her story. She and many of the others had been in Treblinka in Poland. Some of the prisoners she had been traveling with had been stuffed into railcars. The railcars had been filled with chlorine buckets. The intention was to suffocate the prisoners. The train was loaded and moved down the tracks a few kilometers from Treblinka to a forest station. The train cars were opened and the dead bodies were removed and buried by ditches that had been dug by male prisoners. Once the burial was completed, the men who dug the ditches were gunned down.

She continued her story, "My Papa believed the guards in Treblinka when they told him that my mother and sisters were going to a work camp. Thus, he didn't protest when they put my mother and sisters into a truck. I managed to run away. Later, I traded a stolen diamond ring for gentile papers on the black market." She gave me a speech about the good having long since died and the only ones still alive were those willing to do anything to stay alive; that is why she did what she did.

Her escape was an extraordinary story as Treblinka, as a death camp, was as well secured and as busy as Auschwitz II-Birkenau. In Treblinka, during its sixteen months of existence, some 800,000 to 900,000 Jews perished. The camp was shut down in late 1943, after an uprising of prisoners.

"How did you end up back here?" I asked.

She said that a farmer had turned her in, probably for a bounty award. She had tried to pass herself off as a gentile but the Nazis would have no part of the ruse. In any case, at this stage in Nazi madness, some gentiles too were being rounded up for slight infractions, suspicions or maybe for no reason at all. As I listened to her, I could well understand how a heart was able to become so frozen and able to sacrifice a fellow man in order for survival.

CHAPTER TWENTY-THREE

ESCAPE PLAN

AS THE DEFEAT OF THE NAZIS became most certain, it occurred to us that the SS would one day turn on Auschwitz itself: that all inmates would be annihilated and the wretched place set afire, blown up, and bulldozed under so that when the Russians came they would see little to suggest anything more than a benign internment camp.

On October 7th, the entire camp was put on lock down. Prior to the lockdown, I had a nagging feeling that something was about to go terribly wrong. I didn't know why but something seemed off. I started asking around. No one seemed to have enough information to help me figure out what was bothering me. Joli said it was anxiety from being on edge for so long but I knew it was more. It took me over twenty-four hours of questioning everyone before I could I manage to piece together enough information to figure it out.

Niko told me what he knew as he repaired damage to the electric fence. Bayla, who witnessed the massacre, filled in the rest: The twelfth Sonderkommando squad, realizing their time was short, decided that they were not going to be killed without a fight. They had a plan. They began arming themselves. Over several weeks they had stolen, and smuggled into their quarters whatever weapons they could. They had planned a mass escape that would involve overcoming their guards. Knowing that the fence was not always electrified, they carefully planned their timing. Once beyond the fence, they planned to cross the Vistula, which was two kilometers from the outside fence, and run into the forest on the other side. There, they felt they would be safe or perhaps would hook up with partisans that supposedly live in the woods until the war was over.

According to information from Polish underground agents, October 7th was when the SS was scheduled to do their Sonderkommando liquidation thus the day the men planned for the breakout.

The escape plan failed miserably. Apparently, someone had informed the guards, forcing the prisoners to act quickly, too quickly. The men in Crematorium Four prematurely blew up the installation. Those inside Crematorium Two threw an SS soldier and a kapo into the blazing furnace. Thirty Sonderkommando's managed to get to the fence and cut the wires but were gunned down.

The SS secured the remaining buildings before they were destroyed. In all, several hundred Sonderkommando were killed that night. One building was badly damaged and another suffered some damage. A fresh squad of Sonderkommando took the place of the dead and the survivors. The Sonderkommandos that survived the raid were liquidated by being shot with flamethrowers. Their charred remains were trucked back to the crematorium for processing.

The SS kept us standing in roll call formation all day as they took revenge their revenge on the Sonderkommando. We were not taken to the toilets and those with stomach or bladder problems relieved themselves many times over as we stood in ranks, the rest of us held on as long as we could. The stench of human waste combined with the smell from the burning ditch and the crematoria made us all nauseous. As the day wore on, some could no longer stand and fell to the ground.

We were counted over and over again to assure that all tabulations were exact. We knew that we would be kept in roll call until every last person, alive and dead, was accounted for. The electric fences were fully charged. I saw a woman edging toward the fence. I wondered if she was going to run into its open arms. She did; the fence welcomed her warmly as her body wrapped around the wires. It sparked and smoked until little was left of her but a lingering odor of burnt flesh.

Soon after the aborted escape, the crematorium was again ready to resume their gruesome activity. The remnant populations of arriving Eastern European Jews were hurried to their deaths. They poured out of the cattle cars. Very few of those were sent to internment as most were already in poor health. The majority of those Jews had suffered up to five years in wretched confinement. They had experienced extreme deprivation and torture; they were emotionally broken, weakened from starvation, and suffering from various maladies.

During the month of October, the weather grew terribly cold. Roll calls became agonizing as we stood row upon row. Those who had died during the night were thrown in heaps in front of our rows, nothing out of the ordinary. Some of the dead had died open-eyed and open-mouthed, their jaws stretched the thin elastic skin that covered their faces. The rotted or missing teeth gave them a ghoulish appearance. Their dresses were filthy and stained with urine, excrement and often blood. Those that had starved to death had swollen legs and abdomens, patches of peeling skin, and patches of dry and brittle hair. They no longer looked human but like something out of a horror story, which was exactly what we were living.

Those of us still standing were not in much better shape. Our skin was ruptured and scabbed over from our vigorous scratching of the lice and fleas. Runny noses and coughs ran rampant. I didn't know how many of the women had tuberculosis or pneumonia. All of us were severely malnourished but some of us were stronger than others. It seemed that some of the women were simply willing themselves to death.

The population of Lager C was being severely reduced by the day. Whole barracks were emptied overnight. It was but a few minutes' walk to the gas chambers and crematoria. Those marched away barely protested as they took their last few steps. The weeks and months of captivity had paralyzed the nerves and shattered the will. They had experienced the trauma of being yanked from their home; forced into wretched ghettos; stuffed into cattle cars; wrenched from the arms of their families; been herded and shorn like sheep; stockpiled in squalid quarters; inventoried like warehouse goods; abused by sadistic overseers; and often were branded. In their final moments, they were shoved naked into large airtight rooms and forced to inhale prussic acid gases (Zyklon B). Locked inside, they could finally vent their protests with impunity – right up to their last breath.

And who was left to recite Kaddish? Who would mourn them and remember them on earth or in heaven?

CHAPTER TWENTY-FOUR

GOLDIE

THE COLD WINTER DAYS were as vicious as the Nazis. The roll calls were slowly killing Goldie. After a day of standing, snow up to our ankles, I had to carry Goldie's frozen body back to the block. On the bunk, I gave her body a vigorous rubdown to try to warm up her tiny limbs. I took off her shoes and a placed her frostbitten toes in my mouth to bring the feeling back to them. When I sensed a sort of revival in my baby sister, the three of us curled up tightly to each other trying to keep warm. We cuddled together waiting for our few bites of food but it never came. And, while it might not have been much, those few bites kept us going. Something was better than nothing.

It was several hours past our normal feeding and we had resolved that the Nazis had decided that they just weren't going to feed us at all any more. It is not like that would be a surprise. Finally, around midnight, we received our soup. When the cauldron arrived, it was still steaming. It was a huge relief, for everyone. We took turns warming our hands against the sides of the rusted iron pot and in the rising steam. The first swallow of soup was delicious. At that point anything hot would have tasted good. I forced my second swallow on Goldie, although she tried to refuse. I could see she didn't have long if she didn't eat.

Several hours later, the kapos came round again shouting morning roll call. Perhaps a third of the block remained in their bunks. The dead or near dead were carried off for disposal and were quickly replaced by girls from other blocks. It had become a sort of organize chaos as the SS began consolidating inmates as they emptied block upon block.

It was harder now to get information from girls I had known from other blocks and work squads. The Germans were losing the war against the Allies but not against the Jews. The Soviets were about 50 kilometers away from Auschwitz. The trains were arriving less frequently. *Had all the Jews been killed? Were there any Jews left in Europe, or if they were all in Auschwitz?*

With the Red Army advancing on a still resisting Wehrmacht, and Allied planes dropping bombs on the factories nearby, we had reason to hope for our deliverance. Despite the glimmer of hope, I wondered if it would come too late for us.

From Lager C, I could see across the way to the men's camp. Large numbers of men, who had worked for many months, perhaps years, in German factories were now being liquidated in Auschwitz. They were pitiful-looking. Gaunt, dispirited and worn out. They were waiting until a gas chamber could accommodate them. The ground was covered with a thin layer of snow and frost, yet these men were made to stand outside naked. By nightfall they would be dead and hauled away. I strained to see if my Papa or three older brothers were among them. I held my breath as I scanned the group praying I wouldn't see them. I let out a little sigh as my eyes moved over each man and didn't recognize anyone.

We could hear these men moan and cry as we lay in our bunks that night. One of the girls in the barrack began to sing a traditional Jewish lullaby. The rest of us joined in. The singing soothed the darkness. *Were we singing to calm the men or to drown out the sounds from outside? I didn't know.* Auschwitz had a way of making you unsure of your motives. I began to cry. The moans eventually stopped which only could mean one thing.

* * *

I had no idea as to why our block was one of the last to face liquidation. Perhaps it was because Block 24 was located at the end of a long line of blocks, furthest from the crematoria. I wondered why the inmates of other cleared blocks were sent to replace our depleted numbers. Nothing was making sense. The number of girls in our block was maintained at about 4,000 for more than a month. It was a huge change for Lager C, a block that once housed 36,000 female prisoners. I walked on pins and needles trying to figure out what the plan was, or if there was even a plan.

Because we were on curfew most of the time, it became harder and harder to scavenge for food. But, because I needed food for Goldie, I volunteered more often to make the food runs. My heart was breaking watching her already tiny body become smaller and weaker. On the runs to the camp kitchen, I would manage to find scraps. I was fortunate because my contacts among the kitchen inmates were still there after so many months in the camp.

★★

The day finally arrived when there were no longer selections made in our lager. While it gave a reprieve, when anything un-usual occurred it was reason to suspect the worst.

I didn't need to speculate for long as this was only a pause before the final onslaught against the remaining prisoners oc-curred. The doors of our block suddenly flung open, and in charged what seemed like thousands of girls. They were tram-pling over each other as they bulldozed our barrack. Kapos clob-bered them with sticks as they stampeded through the doors. *Was this the last roundup of Lager C? Was the next act by the SS to throw canisters of gas into the block and be done with us, or would we be sealed in to freeze and starve to death?* We all sat locked in the barrack for days, wondering what was going to happen next.

Finally, several SS men and women came into the block and ordered us to undress. We were told to hold our dresses and shoes in our hands and then to exit the block. The orders were repeated over and over while their sticks rained down on us. The Blockova and her kapos were making a big effort to appear efficient in front of the SS. They too knew that this was no ordinary operation.

I ran over to the Blockova and pleaded with her to save Goldie. She screamed at me in Czech, "Dr. Mengele is selecting 800 girls for work and only 800 girls."

There was a fear in her eyes, fear that I had never seen be-fore. Perhaps, now she was nothing more than just another Jew in Auschwitz, expendable, like the rest of us.

Outside of Block 24, the SS had created a human fence be-tween Block 23 and Block 24, so no one could escape. I knew

now that total liquidation had come to Lager C. My survival skills went up into high gear. My heart started pounding so
hard that I could barely hear anything else. Dr. Mengele stood
by the door ordering the Mussulmen and the sick to be lined up
for their final death march. I pushed my way back to where Joli
and Goldie were. If this was a selection for work, as it certainly
seemed it was, I knew the rest of the girls would be sent to the
gas chamber. The block was emptying out fast.

When I reached Joli, I ordered her to get outside and to volunteer for any work squad that was being selected. She resisted.
I gave her a push, "I love you Joli. The time has come for us to
split up. I don't want you to die! If I don't make this work selection, promise me on our Momma's love you will try and take
care of yourself and survive. Please, I beg you, if I am not there
to watch over you, you will not sell your body for food no matter
how hungry you are. Go! Go right now! I will stay with Goldie.
Maybe a miracle will happen and the selection will stop!"

"You must come with me," she cried. "Momma told you to
take care of me, too. Please, I need you just as much as Goldie
does. Please do not go to the gas chamber with Goldie! You
can't!"

I gave her a big hug and kiss.

"Go, they can't kill us all," I said as I pushed Joli towards the
exiting girls.

I had no idea how to save Goldie. My head pounded. I stared
at my sweet little sister. It was basically impossible to escape this
last selection and Goldie knew it better than I did. The fact that
she had survived six and a half months in Lager C was nothing
short of a miracle.

I had once hid her under our bunk to escape a selection. I had dug a hole in the earth's floor and placed her in it. It had worked then; I wondered if it would work again. *What would happen to her when she finally had to emerge from her hiding place?* It was a wild notion but I crawled under the lowest bunk and used my hands to dig the earth even deeper. There was such chaos in the block that no one noticed me digging.

Goldie was crying. I stopped digging. I grabbed her and held her tight. Her little body heaved against mine, "It will be okay. I will save you just like all the other times." I wasn't going to let her go, not because of my promise to my Momma, but because she was my little girl. Because I loved her so much.

I tried to go back to my desperate digging but Goldie pulled me up. She yelled at me to get out of the block and to go with Joli. "If you don't leave me in the block and join Joli, I will simply walk up to the SS and show myself," she said as the tears ran down her face. It was emotional blackmail.

The block was nearly empty. I was afraid that Dr. Mengele would be close to his quota of 800 girls and the selection would be terminated. All not processed would be condemned to death without a chance of passing Dr. Mengele's muster.

"Rifchu, go. You have taken such good care of me. You still have Joli to take care of. She needs you, too."

We hugged and kissed amongst the pandemonium. Tears. I couldn't control my voice, couldn't say a word without shouting it shrilly, "I can't leave you."

Tumult, ferment, agitation. Then Goldie's parting words, "You must leave, Rifchu. You and Joli suffered enough for me. It is not right for you to die with me. Momma does not expect that of you. I suffered enough. It is all over for me. Please go with Joli. I will go and be with Momma."

I held onto Goldie for as long as I could. I don't even know for how long. My little sister, was in a way, like my own child for I had loved her like a Momma would a daughter. As we clung to each other I knew I was risking my life but I couldn't let her go. We had been through so much together. Goldie kept imploring me to leave. She reminded me that I had promised Momma that I would watch over Joli as well.

I wrapped a blanket around her thin shoulders. "Yes, Momma will look for you. I love you! I love you so much!" With that I left, my heart broken in pieces.

Goldie, a child of just over eleven, had the determination of a woman. She accepted the fact that this was the final hour of her life and that when we separated it would be for eternity. We both knew it but Goldie accepted it with far more composure than I could display. It was she who now better fulfilled our Momma's wish that we take care of each other.

I was among the last fifty girls to leave Lager C. Outside, the SS, the Blockovas, and the kapos had formed a corridor to funnel us toward Dr. Mengele and SS-Oberscharfuhrer Irma Grese. Dr. Mengele stood at the head of the corridor. Before him were two SS men. They grabbed the arms of each girl as she approached. Mengele made the final selections – who shall live and who shall die. Those destined to live were sent to Block 23. Those that failed were handed off to SS guards to begin their death march. I wondered if Mengele would recognize me and remember my previous encounters with him. Probably not. He had many confrontations with resisting inmates. Those who had slipped through his noose didn't much bother him because he knew we would all be caught in his net one day. I searched for Joli. As we moved through the corridor of armed guards, it was apparent that there was no way to avoid this selection. Far fewer girls were being sent to Block 23 than to the death march.

Two SS men seized me. I was standing naked before the indifferent eyes of The Angle of Death. His gloved hand motioned me toward Block 23. I would live another day.

Inside the block there was a lot of crying and yelling. I wondered where Joli had been sent. Almost everyone was looking for someone: a sister, friend, or cousin. It was a huge relief when I found Joli. We had a reunion more in relief than celebration. We hugged and cried. We cried for the loss of Goldie, and in relief that we had survived this selection.

We were among the eight hundred women left in the Lager C. I slipped away to make my way towards the fence not far from the lager exit. It was near Block 16 where I saw the group of Lager C girls being marched toward the gas chamber. I got even closer and tried to search the faces of the marchers. The fence stood in my way. *Was I not to have one final glimpse of Goldie?* The marchers shuffled along, their heads down cast, a scene of resignation – the march of the already dead.

Then I saw my little Goldie. She looked more like a Mussulman than the others, perhaps because she was the smallest among them. "Goldie! Goldie!" I yelled. "I love you... I'm sorry. I'm so sorry!.... They took our names. We leave Auschwitz for work..."

She looked up, turned her head. Her face was streaked with tears. Then she saw my frantically waving arms.

"I love you. Work! Go to work!" she shouted. She wasn't ordered to be quiet, just to keep walking faster.

"I love you!" I screamed out the three words I most wanted her to hear. "I love you, Goldie. You will be with Momma. I love you and I always will. Think of Momma. She will be with you. I love you." *Did I really believe that she would be with Momma? No, not really. How could I after watching thousands of girls march to their death? But I wanted her to believe it, to make the end perhaps a bit more bearable.*

The long column moved towards the gray smoke. Goldie's figure blended into the mass of girls and women. Then I caught another glimpse of her just as she turned to look at me. As she did, she stumbled but she did not fall. I hoped for one more sight of her chestnut hair among the sad marchers. As the distance widened, my heart stretched to meet hers.

She was gone from my sight, forever.

I was fixed to the spot where I was standing while Goldie was following the same profaned path into the Valley of Death that Momma, Yidel, Mendel and Pearl had trod six and a half months earlier. My heart was in mourning for all of them. I pitied myself for the love I could no longer express except in memory. And I was angry!

I was angry at God. I raged in my heart against this God, His covenants with His Chosen People; His promise to reward them for their faithful adherence to His law. *What kind of God was this to allow His commandments to be so triumphantly defied? Why did the utterly wicked prosper so completely and for so long? What kind of God did we Jews worship? If He exists, why was He so uncaring of His people; why was He so mute?* I became an atheist.

The long line had disappeared into the maws of the slaughter-house. I tried not to think about what was about to happen to my precious and loving Goldie, but somehow I felt that she would enter the gas chamber without protest. She had witnessed and experienced every cruelty, indignity, privation and fear possible in Lager C. Now, during these last few minutes of her life, I knew this wise child was as noble as any heroine would be in the face of such death. *How would I, so much older than she, have faced my last hour in this place?*

Smoke rose from the crematorium, dispersing yet more Jewish ashes. *Was this the crematorium that had incinerated my Momma and younger siblings? What had become of my Papa and older brothers? Were they still alive, working somewhere in Germany? Or were they too part of some heap of ashes?*

I sunk into the bunk, my heart filled with excruciating sorrow. However, I was also left with a sense of my Momma's love and Goldie's example of courage. I vowed to go on living in spite of the odds.

CHAPTER TWENTY – FIVE

LEFT OR RIGHT

FOR TWO WEEKS, WE, eight hundred remaining women, were kept under lock and key. We were told that we would be leaving for Germany to work in various factories. As a rule, whenever we were in lock down, mass murder was being committed outside our doors. This time was no different. The screams of the innocent played like ambient noise in the outside the walls. The sound of death was all around us and I feared that eventually it would engulf us, too.

To keep some semblance of sanity, we sang songs. We told jokes; we often laughed so hard that we cried. Girls exchanged recipes, not that anyone believed we would ever be able to try them. We told stories from home, some true, some not so true. Some girls talked about how rich and educated they were, even though a blind man could have seen the lies. But who cared. Rich or poor, we were all passengers without life vests on the same sinking ship. We did whatever we could to keep our minds occupied. The days and nights came and went.

Most of the girls were on the edge of sanity when the doors finally opened and we saw the sky. We were told to line up.

Joli was certain that we were going to die, "It's your fault, Edita that I am going to be gassed after all of my suffering. I could have left for a work camp right after we got here. But no, you only wanted to save Goldie. We suffered for nothing. Goldie indeed!"

My temper got the best of me. "I wish I would have let you go! Did anyone guarantee that the first selections were for work? Did anyone offer to organize extra food for you? Did you try to organize any extra food? So far you are alive because I have kept you alive. I did what I believed was the best for you and Goldie. Leave me alone. I have my own guilt to deal with without you giving me a hard time. I promised Momma that I would take care of you and I did everything I could," I said, starting to cry.

We arrived in front of the gas chamber building. We were marched into a large room with white tiled floors and walls. We were ordered to undress and place the clothes in one corner of the room. We were then ordered to line our shoes against another wall and to sit on the floor in one large group.

I felt a large knot in my stomach. *Why did we have to undress and leave our shoes behind?* Something was wrong. I was certain that we were going to be gassed. A group of woman I had met while we worked on the Sonderkommando were coming and going from the room.

"I need to find out what is going on," I whispered to Joli, "I will be right back."

"Don't leave me," she begged.

"I'm not leaving you. I will be right back," I told her.

I scooted my naked butt across the cold tile, navigating between the other bony women, slowly making my way to the group of Sonderkommando's. Call it luck. Call it guts. Perhaps I had a guardian angel watching over me because just as I got to the front, two of the Sonderkommando walked by me. I overheard them speaking in Ukraine, "If the train does not arrive soon, they will all be gassed."

I jumped up, "Please wait. I heard what you said. Please talk to me. We were told that we were leaving for Germany. Can you tell me please what we are waiting for?" When I saw them hesitate, I continued, "Please tell me what you know. I know that you have some information. Are we going to Germany?"

The one woman decided to answer me, "Yes. If the train arrives before 3:00 p.m., five hundred of you will leave for Germany. Three hundred of you will be gassed, that's why you are here in the gas chamber facilities. In the center of the room is a hallway. Dr. Mengele and Oberscharfuhrer Irma Grese are hidden in a nook on the left side. You will not see them until you are in front of them. The door next to them is marked Shower; it leads into the gas chamber. Across from them is another door also marked Shower. If you can go to the right, you might leave Auschwitz. Good luck."

I dropped back down to my bottom and slid my way back to Joli. I told her what I had learned. "Joli, I have a plan. After about three hundred girls go through, you will go. You must not cry. You must stay calm. You must be smart. If you get through, do not trade your body for food or clothing because then you will surely die. I will be about ten girls behind you. Do not look back at me. Remember, I love you. You must do as I say."

Joli protested. I reminded her that thus far I had kept her alive. My intention was to continue to do so. "I will stay behind you so that I can pick a group of skinny girls to follow. Then I will not look so skinny."

At 3:00 pm, I knew the trains must have arrived on time because the selections began. We all rose to our feet, formed a line and began marching forward. I hugged Joli.   Joli did as I told her and she was sent through to the right.

As I approached Mengele's and Grese's hiding place, I was blinded by a bright light. I lost my bearings for a moment but I recovered quickly. As I got closer I feared that one or both of them would recognize me. But there was nothing I could do to avoid them. I finally faced them. I looked him in the eyes; he inspected me as one would a side of meat. He looked at Grese and then back at me. He waved his hand towards the left, towards the gas chamber door. I stood up as straight as I stared him down and screamed at him in German, "Dr. Mengele, I am strong and healthy. I can work, I beg you."

"And what is this?" he asked. He didn't wait for my answer. His right fist flew at my face with the force of his entire body behind him. The impact was so great that I went flying through the door on the right, into the real shower. I realized where I was, I started to scooch deeper into the shower, I felt a hand grab me and pull me inside. It was Joli.

An SS Officer screamed, "Come back here!"

I pushed myself deeper into the crowd of girls who were standing around crying, unsure if they were going to be put to death. Some of the girls understood what was happening and that my life hung in the balance and crowded around me. In the commotion, the girls still waiting outside began to realize what was going on and tried to follow me into the shower room. The

SS became over occupied with trying to hold back the rush of girls. There was no way for the SS to regain order and come after me. I was once again safe.

It wasn't until some calm returned that I felt the pain of Mengele's blow. My lip was split wide open and bleeding. My nose was also bleeding. I began to wonder about what had transpired. *Had Mengele recognized me and that was why he tried to push me to the gas chamber? Had he hit me because of my chutzpa (nerve) to speak to him or was it because he realized I knew the setup and wanted to stop me from saying more? Did it matter at that point?* I had escaped the final selection of Lager C, Auschwitz II-Birkenau. I had survived Auschwitz.

Once all five hundred girls were in the shower, cool water like a summer's rain came down from the ceiling. It felt great. After two months of no showers, not even a trickle of water to wash with this felt like a dream come true. Very quickly the dream came to an end when we were hurried into another room where once again we were shaved and disinfected. Then it was on to a third room that contained long tables covered with dresses and coats. A girl stood behind each table. As we approached, they sized us and gave us a dress. The coat girls did the same. Fortunately, the dresses and coats were different sizes so we traded among ourselves to find clothes that almost fit.

"Shneller, shneller! Rouse, rouse!" "Faster, faster. Out, out," hollered the SS. Without a moment's hesitation, the guards beat anyone who seemed to be dawdling.

We marched to the cattle cars under heavy escort. We took our places as quickly as we could. Bread for each person was tossed into the car and a bucket of water was provided. An empty bucket was also provided to serve as a toilet.

A loud whistle shrieked and very quickly the train got under way. As the train crossed the final switches we were finally leaving Auschwitz behind. I vowed that I would never allow the Nazis to bring Joli or me back to this place of death. We left Auschwitz the same way we had arrived, as human cargo, worthless and highly perishable.

We huddled in the cold car for warmth, both physical and emotional. Though we were clear of Auschwitz, there was no celebrating. We were so dispirited that the prolongation of our lives hardly seemed like a stroke of good fortune. We doubted what was in store for us would be much improvement from where we came from. After all, we had already seen what was done to laborers deemed used up.

The cattle cars held us for several days. Periodically, the doors opened long enough for fresh bread and water to be loaded on and for the waste bucket to be emptied. Much of the time the train stood still. Meanwhile our bodies ached and needed exercise. The car stank. We were getting tired of each other being in such close confinement. Yet, we huddled; huddled out of fear and frigidness.

What struck me as the journey went on was that so many of the railroad stations and tracks appeared to have been damaged or completely destroyed. I couldn't help but wonder again why the railroad station and the tracks into Auschwitz were still intact. *Why hadn't the tracks to and from "the Station of Death" been destroyed? Why was the supply line to Death allowed to function fully when any disruption might have slowed or prevented the murder of thousands?*

CHAPTER TWENTY-SIX

HAINICHEN

AFTER MANY DAYS OF TRAVEL, mostly spent parked on a sidetrack for one reason or another, we came to a screeching halt. The sound of music filled the boxcars. It was joyful and welcoming. *But, what was the point? Why such a greeting for a group of wretched Jewish girls who would be put to work, was it to mock us?*

The doors were pulled open and once again the SS shouted, "Aurstregen" (Disembark). We scrambled to our feet and obediently formed a line. Joli, frightened by the sight of so many civilians, grabbed my hand and held it tight.

Trying to be brave, I responded to her fear, "Do not be afraid. We're out of Auschwitz. It can't possibly be any worse."

Not sure of where we were, I looked around. A metal sign hung above the station building 'Hainichen.' We were in Germany at one of the 100 sub-camps of the Flossenberg Concentration Camps. The forced work camps had become such a pertinent force in the German war industry that they had been divided out so the camps were better utilized. The lost souls at Hainichen worked at an ammunitions factory. Those who proved to be not useful were expendable.

A crowd lined both sides of the street. Hitler youth stood in the street playing their military marching song. An old man in a SS uniform decorated like a Christmas tree held his bayonet like an orchestra conductor. As we stood, SS men and women counted and recounted us. Once the count was complete, the Hitler youth and our SS escorts led us down the street through the town.

We followed behind the music, like rats being led by the Pied Piper of Hamelin. The precession stopped in front of the gates of our new home. The courtyard was dominated by one large two-story building. The larger section of the building housed the prisoners. The smaller section housed an infirmary, kitchen and the SS offices. The camp was surrounded by barbed wire with one lookout post in which an armed guard stood watch. Next door, I could see other buildings occupied by people peeking out of windows.

We were ordered to stop and stand at attention by a beautiful, blond, female SS officer. She introduced herself as the Lagerfuhrerin (camp leader). I understood quickly that she was second in command to the gray-haired SS officer who had led us from the station. We were told to address him as Herr Hauptstrumfuhrer.

The Lagerfuhrerin recited the rules of the camp, what was expected of us and how we were to be punished for infractions. Our labor was to consist of twelve-hour shifts, not including the hour march to and from the factory. We would be working with Russian prisoners of war. There were also going to be German civilians employed at the factory. We were ordered not to talk to or try to communicate with them in any way. Violation of this rule was punishable by death.

While the risk of death was not gone completely at least there were no daily selections, and the rules we had to live by were cut and dry.

An SS officer handed out military style canteens. We got a cup of coffee and a slice of bread before we were ordered to follow the Lagerfuhrerin to the barracks. She assigned half the girls to the top floor and the other half to the bottom floor. The floors were large open spaces. Two rows of bunk beds ran the length of the room. Joli and I ended up on the second floor of the middle section.

Joli and I shared a set of bunk beds. She took the bottom bunk; I took the top. I climbed up the steps and flopped my body down. I sunk down into a straw mattress. My body felt an over-all sense of relaxation to, for the first time in over seven months to not be lying on hard wood. Tiny pieces of the straw would poke through the shabby grey sheets but it sure beat sleeping on the jagged splintering wood. Best of all, there would not be nine other girls lying next to me or feet in my face. The room was also furnished with two wooden tables, and a dozen or so chairs. There was a large industrial style clock on the wall by the entranceway. The minute hand made a loud ticking sound with each time it moved forward, a reminder of how slowly time was passing. But things were better. We may have been treated like prisoners but at least we were living like human beings.

★★★

It was Sunday. Our 'neighbors' strolled the streets of Hainichen, often stopping to look at the work camp. I wasn't sure how much the civilians knew about our existence inside the walls of the buildings. Many of the Germans had been among our welcoming committee at the station. I wondered if they were curious about our clothing, our shorn heads, or our skeletal figures. *Did they know what had happened to us?*

At 4:00 p.m., we were ordered to again assemble in the courtyard. "Line up quietly and orderly. I expect you to behave like civilized people. Those who are disruptive will not receive any rations for the day," a SS guard warned. Withholding food was worse than the smack of a stick. Thus, we rushed outside to the courtyard and stood silent and still.

The Lagerfuhrein began to go through as if we were inventory, deciding who to assign where. She began to pull the stronger looking girls out of line. Joli slid behind me, ducked down, and clutched onto my arms. The Lagerfuhrerin motioned for Joli to come forward. She froze in her spot.

I stepped forward, "I will go, too."

The Lagerfuhrerin nodded.

First shift consisted of thirty-two girls. I being the smallest girl in the group. We were given our instructions: "The morning shift will wake up at 5 a.m., make their beds and line up for breakfast. At 5:30 sharp, the girls selected for the day shift will assemble in the courtyard to begin the walk to the factory garage to pick up the cannons. At 7:00 a.m. sharp, the morning shift will commence work at their assigned workplace. At 7:00 p.m. your work will end and the day shift will line up for the walk back to the camp. SS guards will escort you on your trips back and forth. You will be counted before you leave for work and before the return. If your foreman is German or Russian, you may speak to him only regarding your work. Otherwise, you will speak only when addressed by one of the Officers. If you disobey these rules, you will be severely punished."

"Attention!" screamed the Lagerfuhrein.

The Hauptstrumfuhrer appeared from one of the brick buildings. He was a tall man perhaps in his early sixties. He walked with his hands clasped behind his back. His uniform was neatly pressed; his black boots had a mirror shine. The visor on his cap was pulled down almost to his eyebrows; his eyes focused on us sharply. It was obvious he was about pride and order, and he was going to expect that from us. I feared that many of the women would be punished because most of those who had come out of Auschwitz had lost discipline and self-worth.

Joli and I reported to work the following morning. The Lagerfuhrerin called each of us by our names and told us to step forward. Two SS female guards met us in the courtyard and escorted us on our journey. We walked through the city of the Hainichen in the slushy snow, the cold mush seeping into our wooden shoes. We were still wearing the clothes we had left Auschwitz in and they weren't doing much to defend against October's frosty bite.

We finally arrived to the factory garage. We were escorted inside. While it wasn't much warmer, we were at least out of the elements. That was enough to be thankful for, at least for the moment. Inside the garage were hundreds of cannons, lined up like soldiers, one after another.

The manager from the factory came and greeted us. He walked us towards the cannons. We were told that we would be broken up into teams of eight girls. Each team would be pushing a cannon to the train station. The Nazis were going to use a human team rather than horses or trucks to haul their weaponry.

My team and I pushed our cannon out the large garage door and headed towards the train station. My legs were already weary from the hour walk but I knew that I had better suck it up and find the strength because I had a long day ahead of me. The snow began to fall more rapidly. Icy flakes blew under my dress. Having not been given underwear or stockings, my body chilled in no time. My frozen legs felt like I was walking on wooden stilts. *Suck it up!* I told myself.

It wasn't long into our hauling that we came to a hill, a very large hill. My heart sank. Tears ran down the faces of my teammates.

"One step at a time," I said out-loud. I wasn't sure if I was saying that to them or me but as a team we began moving forward, although, our efforts seemed futile.

Each step we took seemed to get us further behind. We were in a losing battle against the icy road and the slick bottoms of our wooden shoes. As the inclines increased we began slipping, falling and scraping the skin on our legs. Warm sticky blood began running down the tears in my skin. The cannons were sliding all over the road, dragging us with it. Each team struggled to move forward.

The train station was in sight, just one more hill standing in our way. This was going to prove to be our toughest opponent. Here we also had an audience. Several SS guards and civilians stood in the streets laughing at our struggles. We stood in place trying to run the cannons up the hill but we got nowhere. After the SS had their laugh, they doubled up our teams and we finally managed to pull the cannon over the hill and into the station. I now knew why so many of the slave laborers returned to Auschwitz happy to face the gas chambers.

On our return to the courtyard, we were given time to go, unescorted, to the toilets which we shared with the Russian prisoners. An eight-foot high wall divided the men and women's bathroom but there was an open space near the top between the bathrooms. Near the entrance was a sink where we could wash our hands. This was a new luxury, something that we didn't have in the death camps. I used the sink to wash off my bloody legs and hands.

Between the openings of the rooms, I heard the Russian men speaking. I knew that whatever information I could find out was beneficial. I didn't want an infraction so to hide my disobedience I sang the melody of a popular Russian song, changing the words to inquire about our workplace. The Russian prisoner realized what I was doing and responded back to me in song. He told me that we were the first group of women to be used in the prisoner work force. The voice proudly told me that his comrades were pushing forward and that the war would be over soon. I wasn't elated by the information. I had been hearing this for months. I feared that the end would never come in time for Joli and me. I thanked the Russian man and left.

***

The second day was worse. Exhausted and bruised from the first day everything was compounded the next. The heavy snow from the night turned into heavy slush. The cannons either slipped on ice hidden under the slush or got stuck in the thick snowy mush. If we thought the first trip of the day was torture, the afternoon trip was murder. Our wet clothes were frozen stiff, as were our legs and arms. The cannon tires became killers as they rolled over our feet. The injured would scream from pain but no one cared.

As much as Joli was larger and stronger than I was physically, mentally she had broken down. She cried non-stop. Part of me regretted volunteering to work this job. However, I knew that without me, Joli would not be able to contain her hysteria and the SS would be waiting for her with their clubs.

On our return to our room, I debated if I should eat my soup or warm my feet in it and eat it afterwards. I rubbed Joli's hands and feet to get her warm and to try ward off frostbite. I laid down next to her so we could combine what little body heat we had in a desperate attempt to warm up. Joli shivered and in a far-away voice, repeated over and over, "Edita, think of a way to get us out of here."

The next morning, we woke to the roads covered with ice. The cannons slid across the ice tossing us about like rag dolls. It took all of our energy to keep the cannon from falling into the ditch that ran alongside the road. We knew that we could pay with our lives if we destroyed their precious cannon.

We held on to the cannons for dear life while the tears of fear froze to our cheeks. The freezing wind felt like a thousand needles being thrown at our faces. The metal of the cannon became so cold I was certain that I my skin would freeze to it and tear away when I removed my hands.

The fourth day came. We were so tired that we felt that the cannon we were pulling weighed twice as much as the ones before. We were falling even where the road was level. Our scabs reopened and blood flowed down everyone's legs and arms.

Streams of red rivers flowed down the icy paths. When we finally got to the hill, we tried in vain to pull it up and over the top. It was of no use. Our beaten and battered bodies had been through enough. Now it wasn't an issue of going forward but not rushing backward. I noticed that a blond SS woman was watching me. She was not laughing along with the others.

At that moment, my body gave out. I was no longer able to push forward but I knew the cannon couldn't roll back, no matter what. Without thinking there was a chance I could be crushed, I volunteered to lie down in the road behind the cannon to keep it from slipping backwards. I let go of my rope, got out of line and laid down behind the cannon. The blond SS woman realized what I was doing. She rushed over to me and yanked me up from the ground.

"What are you doing, child? You could be killed!" she said, seeming panicked. Before I could explain she ordered the teams to double up so we could get the cannons over the top of the hill and to the train station without such a struggle.

Later that afternoon, while I was washing my hands I felt a tap on my shoulder. I turned around to find myself face-to-face with the SS woman who had kept me from being crushed. She scared the hell out of me.

"Have no fear, I am SS Officer Dali," she said. "What is your name?"

I answered in German, "My name is Edita."

"Oh, you speak German."

"Yes," I answered, "I learned it in the Czech school."

"This is a very hard job for someone so petite and young," she responded.

"Yes it is. But one must do what she must do to survive," I said.

"You look rather German or Slovenian. How did you end up among the Jewish group?" she asked.

I thought for a moment. I could lie, only I knew she would find out, and she seemed so friendly. I decided that the truth was the best lie, "Officer, the fact is that I am Jewish. My family paid with their lives for being Jewish." She made a sound but said nothing at first.

"Before you leave this evening, I will give you my leftovers. I am sure you are hungry," she said. I stood, frozen, unsure of how to respond to this kind SS woman.

"Yes I am. Thank you so much. I hope you won't mind if I share them with my younger sister," I said back.

"You have a sister here?"

"Yes, she is in my group. She is also blond like me," I answered.

"Not this time, no sharing. I want you to eat it all. You are very small and you need the food," she ordered.

"Thank you. I will do as you wish. I would like to reciprocate your kindness. I am a good seamstress. I could make you a blouse or a skirt if you bring me some material, a needle and thread, a tape measure and a pair of scissors," I spoke boldly. I was surprised at my own boldness. My goal, by providing extra services, was to get lenient treatment and maybe some extra rations for Joli and me. This was the first of my encounters with this decent SS woman.

The next morning at first assembly, the Lagerfuhrerin told me that I was being transferred to a work squad inside the factory warehouse. Joli protested and demanded that I not leave her and the team pushing the cannons. It wasn't her choice, or mine. We both marched to the factory but parted ways when we got there. I was given a job cleaning floors in the factory. It was a much easier job.

That night after work, SS Officer Dali came to my room bringing with her the materials and supplies to make her a blouse and skirt. I took measurements and we discussed styles. She proved to be as good as my first impressions of her. She told me that whenever she was on my shift she would give me her leftovers. I was also free to join the groups she escorted to the toilets. "It will do you some good to get a breath of fresh air during the day," she said.

Her kindness gave me courage. I took the opportunity to explain why I wanted to share my food with my sister. "As far as I know, I have lost my whole family except my sister. Before Momma was killed, I promised to take care of her, not knowing I would have trouble taking care of myself. Please, can you help me to get my sister work inside the factory? Please forgive my boldness. Please, if you can," I said with tears in my eyes.

"You are a good sister. You must be a very caring person to share your extra rations, even when you could have eaten them and more," she gave me a smile but said nothing more. The next morning, Joli was assigned to work inside the factory in a different section than me.

This favorable turn of events naturally gave me hope. However, one cold Sunday morning these hopes were suddenly shattered. We were in line in the courtyard. Something unusual was going on as both shifts were assembled. The Lagerfuhrerin paced the length of the lines, glaring at us. She stopped halfway in front of our formation and yelled, "The girl who accepted the comb from a German citizen come forward."

No one moved. The SS woman pointed to a girl from the night shift and ordered her to come forward. When she did the Lagerfuhrerin smacked her across the face causing the girl's nose to bleed. "The comb!" the Lagerfuhrerin said, extending her hand to receive it.

The girl cried as she pulled the comb from her dress pocket. The Lagerfuhrerin held the comb high like a trophy, "You will be punished. Kneel to receive your punishment."

The girl dropped to knees. She fell forward into the snow, pleading for the Lagerfuhrerin to forgive her. Her words were a waste. The Lagerfuhrerin kicked the girl in the stomach, causing her to double over. As the poor girl screamed, the Lagerfuhrerin kicked her some more. The Lagerfuhrerin's boots were bloody. The snow began to turn pink then red. The Lagerfuhrerin pulled out her gun and shot the girl. Her body was quickly carried away.

The Lagerfuhrerin collected herself, adjusted her clothing, and turned her attention to the assembled prisoners who were aghast their spots. She was satisfied that her deadly deed made a profound impression on us. She dismissed us to get our food. It was a quiet meal. I don't think any of us were as horrified about the death, we were used to that. We were horrified that we had thought we were safer now, and those hopes were shattered with a single gunshot.

***

Two days later the SS had gathered both work shifts in the courtyard. They had us waiting longer than usual without being addressed. This couldn't be a good sign. The Hauptstrumfuhrer, two high ranking SS Officers, a German civilian and the factory foreman finally appeared, I was sure that one of the girls was going to pay. The Hauptstrumfuhrer was leading the way. They walked slowly, zeroing in on each person, stopping now and then. They were like lions stalking their prey. I knew they weren't looking for me, however, I held my breath anyways.

After eyeing every girl in our work squad the SS stopped to have a brief discussion before coming back to me. My heart stopped. *What had I done?* No matter, I stood tall looked them in the eyes and refused to show fear, although I was shaking in my boots.

The Hauptstrumfuhrer asked me to step forward. I walked forward slowly, visualizing my death.

"What is your name?" he asked.

"My name is Edita Kalus," I answered in German.

"You speak German, that is good." he responded. "Can you tell me about your education?"

"I graduated high school," I answered.

"What was your favorite subject?" was the next question.

"Math and History," I responded, curious why they cared about what subjects I liked in school.

"Come with us," he ordered.

I gave a farewell glance to Joli before following them to a SS Offices. They led me into a building that the prisoners were told we were never allowed to enter. Signs read PRIVATE. DO NOT

ENTER. The Hauptstrumfuhrer opened the door to a conference room. It was finely decorated. A large wooden conference
table and twelve oversized leather chairs sat in the middle of the
room. They all sat down, like we were about to have a typical
business meeting. I stood at attention in an attempt to hide my
shaking.

"Have a seat," the Hauptstrumfuhrer said.

I must be dreaming.

"I hope that you have good ears and your mind is like a
sponge," the Hauptstrumfuhrer said. I nodded, unsure of what
he wanted from me. The Hauptstrumfuhrer explained that I was
going to be taught engineering work by SS Officer Ader and the
German civilian engineer, Mr. Spar. They were both skilled engineers and would be responsible for overseeing my output; I was
going to be building replacement parts for trucks, and gearing
pistons for cars and airplanes. I was to learn how to distinguish
good parts from bad parts.

"I must warn you. The machine you will use pumps oil from a
reservoir located in the basement. The oil lubricates a drill that
cuts and polishes the product; the oil returns through a filter in
the machine to the reservoir. Oil is more precious than gold. It
is imperative to clean the machine daily because any shavings
could clog the machine," the Hauptstrumfuhrer explained.

I hung onto every word but what I couldn't figure out was
why I was being given this job. I received a green cotton dress
and a yellow plastic coat to protect me from the spurts of oil that
came from the cutting drill used to finish the product.

My training was to commence immediately. I followed SS
Ader to the factory. He taught me how to use hone heads that

had the capacity to measure to the thousandth of a millimeter. He told me that there are to be twelve holes in each cylinder mounting and they must measure exactly to the same millimeter apart. While the work required precision, I had a bit of leeway; if one hole was off, I could retool for one of two other sizes. I was reminded that the civilian engineer would check my completed products.

For almost two weeks, SS Ader drilled the various aspects of my job into me. I feared that I would never learn everything and that the job would cost me my life. Whenever I seemed to catch on, it seemed as if my SS teacher worked harder to mess me up.

At the end of the two weeks, the Mr. Spar reprimanded SS Ader for misleading me. When SS Ader walked away, he said "Do not worry, I will teach you what you need to know. He is leaving tomorrow for the front. He was deferred from the army to work on this machine. Your learning how to run this machine frees him to serve at the front."

I hoped that maybe, just maybe, I had a guardian angel in this old engineer. It was the kind, old German gentleman who taught me the process of producing the mounting for the equipment cylinders. I did ruin a few pieces in the processes of learning and whenever I did he would quickly take it and place it in the garbage can in the next room. The Hauptstrumfuhrer often stopped by my machine to check on my progress. I believed that Mr. Spar had praised my work. In return for my efforts, I received a slice of bread with my dinner.

The war was getting closer to Hainichen. There were occasional air raids but nothing touched us. During the raids, we were all escorted downstairs into the basement bunker. The

Jewish prisoners and the POW's were on one side of the room and the Germans on the other. The Lagerfuhrerin warned us that anyone who attempted to escape during a raid would immediately be put to death.

The nearing presence of the Allies caused a decrease in food for the slave labor as our designated food allotment wound up in the mouths of civilian refugees. The quality of the food that we were given also decreased drastically. And, just as our nourishment was decreasing our workload was increasing. We were working as if the very war depended on it.

It was getting much colder now that December's weather had arrived. Many of the girls grew ill due to the long days of labor and the reduced rations. Every day, a few more girls were carried back to the camp and packed into one of the isolated rooms that held eight beds. Most suffered from bad colds, high fevers and bad coughs. Joli and I were lucky to have jobs indoors so we were better off than most of the girls that were coming down with severe illnesses.

★★★

I enjoyed the days that SS Officer Dali was on duty at the factory. She was usually lenient about the amount of time I was away from my machine. Dali would give me permission to take a break whenever she took a group to the toilets. She wanted me to clear my lungs from the fumes of the hot oil and other grime and soot of the factory.

The days were monotonous. I felt like I was killing time waiting to be freed. The loneliness of being trapped in one place doing the same thing over and over gave way too much time to replay the past year over and over. One particularly cold and dreary day, I was lost in thought when Dali came to get me for a bathroom break. It was good timing. I needed to clear my head.

I was in the bathroom, splashing water on my face, when I remembered - I left my machine running! I raced back to my station without an escort. To my horror, oil was running out of the machine. A large puddle had formed underneath the machine and oil was flowing in every direction. There was nothing I could do. I sat down, afraid and helpless. I had been warned about wasting oil. I saw myself marked as a saboteur. There would be a public hanging or some other execution performed by the Lagerfuhrerin.

As I sat there forlorn, a small crew of Russian POW's appeared with wheelbarrows and sawdust. They quickly spread the sawdust on the oil. In a matter of minutes the sawdust and slurped up oil and the Russians were able to shovel it off the floor and carry it away. My guardian angel, Mr. Sabar, had come to my rescue again. To cover my mistake, he had broken the pipe that returned the oil to the reservoir.

Quietly, but angrily, he warned me to be careful not to leave my machine running unattended again. He chided me about how lucky we both were not to have been caught in my neglect and his cover-up. I knew he would have been powerless to prevent punishment if I had been caught and he would have been punished as well.

After Dali had finished escorting prisoners to the toilets, she came to me and warned me about being careless with my machine. She told me that she would not report me.

Thank you, Momma! Thank you, Goldie!

CHAPTER TWENTY-SEVEN

SASHA

"**H**ello," a voice said in Russian.

There was a tall, blond, blue-eyed Russian POW behind me. The Russian worked on the opposite side of the factory, about one meter from my station. We had caught each other's eyes from time-to-time but I never dared to speak to him. I stood there in silence between my freshly cleaned station and the Russian.

"My name is Sasha, I was born in Moscow," he said politely, "What is your name? Why are you among the Jewish prisoners? You don't look Jewish."

I contemplated not answering. I knew that was the smart thing to do. I already had one major infraction for the day but I hated being told that I didn't look Jewish. "Yes, I am a Jew. I look like myself. How are Jews supposed to look? Are we supposed to have horns?" I asked in Russian.

"I apologize. I didn't mean anything by my comment. I am surprised you speak Russian," he said.

Sasha told me that he had wanted to write me notes and give me food but hadn't been sure I could read or speak Russian. He continued talking to me and asking questions but I was scared thus I tried my best to make it seem like he was doing the fraternizing and I was innocent in the exchange. It was a good thing I did because it wasn't long before Mr. Sabar passed by. He motioned for Sasha to walk away.

"Until we meet again, Edita," Sasha said, tipping his hat. I said nothing.

That evening Sasha left an extra piece of bread by my machine as a gift.

Sasha became a fast friend. This ended up becoming rather fortunate as Russian prisoners received much more food than Jewish prisoners and he was more than happy to share with me.

The Russians also had the ability to work overtime and earn credits at the factory store where they could purchase a variety of items. Sometimes, I would find an apple or a boiled potato at my station. Sasha found a way to smuggle in a pair of heavy shoes for me to replace the sabots that I had been given the day that I had arrived in Auschwitz. I didn't put the shoes on right away; I hid them behind my machine fearing that I would be punished for accepting them. At the urging of the Mr. Sabar, I put on the shoes. Mr. Sabar threw my sabots away. The shoes were a great relief to the sabots that I had been wearing.

Communications occurred somewhat easily in the toilet room. I could clearly hear what was being said on either side of the wall. That is where I was able to pick up information about the progress of the war. The Russians had an information pipeline to the outside world; I never learned how it worked.

It was in the toilet room that Sasha and I were able to talk. Most often we communicated by notes. His notes often were concealed inside the bread he smuggled me. When our work shifts differed, he arranged for another prisoner to get me the bread. It was so nice to have someone to talk to, to share my feelings to without worry or guilt.

***

The day after Christmas, I returned to the camp from the factory. Joli was nowhere to be found. She had been spending her work hours in a different part of the factory packing parts so our paths never crossed during the day. I searched everywhere for her. Finally, I found out that she had taken ill and was transferred to the camp dispensary. When I got to the dispensary, she was in severe pain, huddled in a ball and crying. I had never seen her ill before, not even in Auschwitz. I held her hand and told her that I was going to stay with her as much as I could.

At my next shift, I pleaded with the Hauptstrumfuhrer for permission to work the night shifts so I could be with Joli during the day. Because I had proven myself in the factory, he gave me permission to change to the night shift. Each morning, after I finished my shift, I got a cup of coffee and went to Joli's bedside. I would hide some of the food I received from Sasha under my dress and smuggle it into the dispensary for Joli. Whenever I was able, I also gave some of the extra food for the other girls in the dispensary. While I sat with Joli, I would work on sewing clothing for SS Officer Dali, hoping to receive even more food to share.

Meanwhile, the air raids were becoming much more frequent causing constant disruption at the factory. Each time a siren sounded, we were hustled into the basement along with all other prisoners, civilians and guards. The Germans were having a hard time holding back the advancing Russians.

In January, the Lagerfuhrerin was getting more and more sadistic, meting out punishments for both real and fictional infractions. She was much like the runaway cannons.

Having broken every rule, I feared that one day she would run me over. I knew that the Lagerfuhrerin had her eyes on me. I only hoped that it was because she knew of the extra privileges I had been receiving.

"You are a special worker in this factory, the only one that we have been able to train on this machine and have earned your worth with the extra work you do. That is what I tell them when they get all up in arms," Dali told me, kindly.

The following week the Lagerfuhrerin called for both shifts to assemble on the second floor for a lice check. She paced in front of us with her whip in hand, slapping it against her black boots. It was obvious she was in the mood to stomp on someone. There were half dozen shearers ready to check for lice and shave our heads if they found anything. They were situated behind a long table that stood as a boundary between "us" and "them." We were relieved when Laerfuhrerin stopped her marching and took a seat on the other side of the table with the shearers.

Each girl approached one by one. The occasional girl needed her head shaved, but it was nothing like the infestation that ran rampant in Auschwitz. While no one had long hair, there was blatant relief when each girl was able to keep their short-cropped hair. As my turn to approach the girl assigned to checking my hair, the Lagerfuhrerin gave me a particularly long, angry look.

My inspector pronounced me clean of lice. Phew! While it wasn't much, I was so glad to have the coating of blonde fuzz covering my bald scalp. The fresh hair reminded me of the growing grass in spring. To have it taken away again would have been devastating. I turned to take my place back in line, when the Lagerfuhrerin's voice pierced my ears, "Halt! Remain where you are."

At first I wasn't sure if she was speaking to me. I had no idea what she had caught me doing. I slowly turned my head towards the frigid woman. She must have seen the uncertainty in my eye because before I could ask her anything she barked, "Yes, you, Edita. Stand at attention, right where you are at."

I remained in front of the assembly until the inspection concluded. Once everyone had their heads checked the Lagerfuhrerin sat down at the table. She picked up her whip and began stroking it through her hands. Then, still sitting, she banged the table several times with the end of the whip. Everything became still and silent, even the wind hushed to her command. She ordered me to approach her. I stepped within six feet of the table and resumed my stance at attention.

The Lagerfuhrerin rose from her chair and announced to the crowd, "Edita's hair is to be shaved off even if she doesn't have lice. I have received information from the night shift guards that she plans to escape during an air raid, posing as a German."

I had wasted oil by being negligent. I had talked to Russian prisoners. I had received and written notes. I had received Russian shoes. I had smuggled extra food into the camp. I had broken almost every rule there was, I would take my punishment. I would not take a punishment for a fabricated misdeed.

I knew why she said what she did. The Lagerfuhrerin could hardly suppress her hatred for any prisoner that had blond hair who spoke the same tongue as her Fuhrer and could pass as a member of the master race. She took such prisoners as a personal reproach to her. I knew that she would humiliate me before she beat me or killed me. She stared at me, triumphant and mocking, waiting for me to beg for mercy, to admit to her lies. Such actions were a turn-on for her and helped her work herself into a violent rage.

"Come closer, you filthy Jew!" she screamed.

I stepped closer to her, "Lagerfuhrerin, you could put a cross on me that lights up in the dark just like the ones the Russian prisoners wear. I could wear a handkerchief to cover my hair. You do not have to remind me that I am your prisoner. I am fully aware of it. I am also aware of your power over me. I believe that you know that I have no intention of trying to escape. I have lost all of my family except for my sister who is here. Before my Momma was sent to her death in Auschwitz, I promised her that I would take care of her. I know that you are aware that my sister has been very sick for several weeks and has been in the infirmary. Do you believe that I would leave her and break the last promise I made to my Momma? If you have made up your mind that I am guilty, then go ahead and kill me, you would be doing me a favor. Only don't cut off my hair or kick me to death. I have worked hard in your factory at night and have sewn clothes for you and your friends during the day. I *deserve* a bullet from you."

The Lagerfuhrerin jumped up and interrupted my speech with a hard crack across my face. "You pig, you stupid pig! Do you know with whom you are speaking to? You are my prisoner." She paced back and forth more quickly, slapping her palm with her whip. She kept repeating, "Do you know who you are speaking to?"

As she continued to pace, she made a fist but didn't deliver a blow. Instead, she returned to her chair at the table and slammed down her whip. Her voice had a tinge of hesitation, "You are my prisoner and I can do anything I want with you."

"Your sewing and your so-called good work at the factory are your duties. You are a German prisoner. You are just a dirty Jew." Her rage seemed to subside. I wondered if I should talk some more. However, before I could open my mouth, she got up again and started to look me up and down. I hadn't the faintest idea what she was up to. I feared that she would notice the shoes that I was wearing.

"Who gave you those stockings?" she asked pointing to my legs.

"I cannot tell you," I said politely.

"Who? Give me her name," she demanded. Her rage seemed to be returning. She slapped my face. "Give me her name," she screamed.

"One of your SS women friends gave them to me. I was assured that it was alright to accept them," I responded. "It was a good deed and I cannot betray such a fine person because she was kind to me."

"Would you rather die than tell me her name?" she asked mockingly.

I gambled and answered, "Yes, I would rather die. You've made up your mind to do away with me one way or another. Why should I cause a kind person trouble?" I was so afraid that she would focus on the shoes next.

Perhaps I took this tactic with the Lagerfuhrerin because, for some unknown reason, I really didn't believe that she would carry out her death threat. Somehow, I was convinced that had I broken down, had I pled for mercy, or had I shown fear, I would have been doomed. Somehow, I felt I understood her and I was grateful that I had the presence of mind to act on my feelings. She was a bully whose weapon gave her strength. Perhaps something in her prevented her from killing someone possessing the qualities admired in the master race, even a Jew.

The long stand-off between the Lagerfuhrerin and I was interrupted by a shout from the assembly, "Please Lagerfuhrerin, do not kill her."

Some said I was a good person; some said I was kind. While I appreciated the support, I worried that the pleas would only infuriate her even more. A chorus went up: "Don't kill her. Don't kill her." As I listened to the girls, I knew that my Momma had been right when she had told me that when you are good, goodness would be repaid in spades. Only, I worried that the girls would also be punished.

In any case, the Lagerfuhrerin made no attempt to stop the noisy demonstration, nor did the other SS standing nearby. It seemed as though the Lagerfuhrerin was enjoying all the fuss, even though it was prisoners protesting her actions.

"She must be punished," the Lagerfuhrerin repeated over and over. I took this to mean that she needed a way to save face.

I pulled my last card, hopefully my ace of spades, "Frau Lagerfuhrerin. I have had special training by two engineers on the proper way to run a very special machine. I am the only one trained and was the only one of five hundred girls who could learn the proper process. The factory manager and the Haupt-strumfuhrer will inquire as to why I am not working at the machine. I can assure you that the product I am making is vital to the war effort."

"I have heard enough!" she interrupted. She slapped me, "I asked you to give me the name of the woman who gave you the stockings. If you do not tell me, you will die."

From the assembly came a shout, "I will tell you."

The Lagerfuhrerin slapped me again and ordered the girl to come forward.

"Please don't come. You will be killed, too," I yelled without turning around. I feared that what she said would only make matters worse.

The girl stepped forward and identified, "SS Dali" as the source of the stockings. I quickly interjected that the stockings were for the extra work I did for SS Dali, work that the Lager-fuhrerin knew about. I was slapped again and told to shut up. She then ordered the girl to go back to her place in the assembly, but not before she gave the girl a hard slap, too.

The Lagerfuhrerin seemed to run out of steam. She went back to her chair, a kind of retreat. Nothing was said for several minutes. I kept my mouth shut. The whole mad scene petered out just like that, like a bad play, one in which the audience leaves in utter confusion. All I knew was that I had once again somehow survived a death threat.

CHAPTER TWENTY-EIGHT

THE PROMISE

DURING THE LONG DARK NIGHTS at the machine I would try to drive away my sadness by singing softly to myself. The noise level in the factory was so high that it eliminated the chance of neighbors overhearing my song and telling me to stop.

We were a self-contained unit and most everyone did their job so there was not much interference by factory officials hustling us along. There were also few disturbances from the SS guards. The work we were performing required concentration and was regarded as important so interruptions were kept to a minimum. It was an unusual experience to be left alone by the SS. I credited the lax in supervision to the fact that we were meeting quotas and the Nazis felt they were getting as much out of us as they were likely to get. We were fortunate that our factory officials realized that it was costly to work prisoners to complete exhaustion and death.

The long hours and tedium made the work very hard, especially because we were grossly underfed. Occasionally, we would receive extra rations. The SS were only interested in maximizing efficiency; keep the trained prisoners alive with the minimal amount of expenditures. For as long as the Jews were serving the Reich, they would survive. Once their usefulness was over, death was certain.

★ ★ ★

There were nights that the darkness would eat me alive. The singing would soothe my soul. One particularly sad night I felt a tap on my shoulder. It was the Hauptstrumfuhrer. Before I recovered from my surprise, he greeted me with a pleasant, "Good evening."

I jumped up from my stool, turning off the machine, and stood at attention.

"Sit down, sit down child and continue your work," he said with a friendly smile. He stood watching me operate the machine. I became nervous. *Why was I getting this special attention from the highest ranking SS officer in the camp? Why was he calling me child? Was he going to take advantage me?*

In the days that followed, he made similar visits, greeting me in a friendly manner and complimenting my work. It was quite in contrast to the style and manner of his subordinate, the Lagerfuhrerin.

One day he stopped to ask me about my work, my age, where I came from, and other such personal questions. I was very circumspect in my answers. I couldn't help but wonder why he was stepping out of the normal character of an SS officer. While I never saw him punish anyone himself, he never stepped up and stopped the brutality of the other guards and the Lagerfuhrerin. I couldn't completely trust him or even SS Dali who never gave me any reason to distrust or fear her. My nervousness increased each time he made a friendly overture. I decided that I would not let my guard down but I would play the good, polite Jewish prisoner.

I filled another night with song and tears when the Hauptstrumfuhrer came to visit me again, "How is it you can sing and cry at the same time?" he asked without mockery. He followed that question with another. "What language is that?" He then took his finger and wiped a tear off my cheek.

I felt immediate fear. *What was he doing? Was he lulling me in a sense of safety only to then sadistically hurt me?*

Perhaps it was all of the pent-up feelings I was having, but in that moment I broke down. I burst out, "It is a Hungarian love song my Momma sang to us our last day in the ghetto. I am afraid to return to the camp because the Lagerfuhrerin seems determined to kill me. My sister is ill and is getting worse. I don't know why I am telling you this. I only want my sister to live. She's all I have."

The unconnected recitation of my miseries came out spontaneously and as quickly as it came out I wish I inhaled back in. The Hauptstrumfuhrer seemed to recognize that I was beside myself.

"What is wrong with your sister?" he asked.

"I don't know."

"Do not give up hope," he replied, his face sincere.

He returned to the subject that seemed to preoccupy him.

"The war will be over soon and I will be your prisoner," he said.

It was such an odd comment. I had no idea how to respond.

"Why are you telling me this?" I asked.

"I was an officer in World War I, commissioned by Hauptstrumfuhrer Heinrich Himmler. I came into the Army to help serve my country. Not to do 'this.' I am a gentleman. I didn't do anything to stop it. I should have done more. I never murdered any of your people. I never, with my own hands, brutalized any of your people. But I should have done more. I will do whatever it takes to make sure you survive. Whatever it takes."

The Hauptstrumfuhrer gave me reason to hope that we prisoners just might survive the last desperate weeks of a chaotic and disintegrating Nazism.

What clouded my brain most was why this old aristocrat decided to befriend me, a member of a people most detested by the SS. On another level, I was almost ashamed that I had listened to such a confession by an officer of the monstrous SS. I asked myself if his title as Hauptstrumfuhrer carried any real power in the Hainichen camp. If it did, why didn't this self-proclaimed gentleman put a stop to the grotesque actions of the lesser officers and guards? *Was he deluded? Was I really under the protection of the top officer of the camp?* Or, was he merely a figurehead who had no more than symbolic power and whose orders could be ignored? I wondered if my life was in greater danger because I seemed to be favored by the Hauptstrumfuhrer. I couldn't reconcile the disparity between the civilized behavior of this man and the atrocious deeds of his underlings. It seemed absurd that the Hauptstrumfuhrer and Dr. Mengele could both be members of the same SS. The only conclusion I could reach was that the Hauptstrumfuhrer was a misfit, a freak in an SS officer's uniform. If Himmler knew what was going on in this man's head, I doubt that the old man would survive the day.

A month passed. It seemed that most evenings, the Hauptstrumfuhrer was waiting to talk to me. When we spoke, he went on about how poorly things were going with the German armies. I wondered what he was up to. Didn't he realize that such talk, especially by an SS officer, was treason? He would discuss how our fates were intertwined – something I didn't understand, but never argued.

"I promise to save your life, if in turn you save mine," he said without a smile.

"I am confused Herr Hauptstrumfuhrer. I believe that a man in your position could protect me and perhaps save my life. But, how can I save yours?" I asked fearfully. I still did not trust him even though he had been nothing but good to me. Not only had he arranged for extra rations for me but he also arranged for me to wash up once a week. On Sundays, I would come to the rear of the SS quarters that were next to ours; someone gave me a bucket of warm water in which I was able to use to wash. Yet, I continued to fear him.

In response, he said, "Listen, and listen well. The war will be over before six weeks pass. As the Russians progress, we will head for the Crimean front. You know, I never raised my hand to anyone. I tried to help you with whatever I could. I want you to be my friend. And, when you are free and I am a prisoner, please tell my captors I did not hurt anyone."

"I must admit that you have been nice to me. I am grateful for the extra bread and the warm water to wash in. But, I need to know how you could let the Lagerfuhrerin beat two girls to death and let her threaten to kill me just because I have blond hair and can speak German," I continued on without letting him respond. "You were very nice to help me. However, before I help you I first have a request, Herr Hauptstrumfuhrer. I told you when you found me crying, that I was worried about my sister. She is the only one of my family of eleven that is left. She has been ill for over two months, living in a cold dormitory. She badly needs to see a doctor, not a girl who claims to be a nurse. Have my sister brought to the doctor here in the factory. I know that the Russians get medical treatment there. If you don't, I won't tell your captors that you were a nice and good German. I can't disappoint my Momma." I never blinked an eye, looking straight into his face, and spoke without fear.

"I'm sorry child. Jews cannot be treated medically," he responded.

"You are in charge of the camp. You must have some authority over the factory doctor and can have him examine her. I have never asked for anything for myself. But now I beg you, help me keep my promise to my Momma who asked me to watch over my sister," I pleaded.

"You are asking for something that is impossible," he responded, and then he left.

I feared going back to the camp. I was certain that in my desperation to save Joli's life I had overstepped my boundaries. I had made demands of the highest-ranking SS officer. My Momma was right, *think before you speak,* she always said to me. Not only had I put myself at risk, but also I feared that I might have become the instrument of Joli's death.

When I got back to the camp and lined up for roll call, the Lagerfuhrerin came and pulled me out of the line and instructed me to report to her office immediately. I was scared to death.

As soon as I entered, she said, "I know that you spoke to the Hauptstrumfuhrer."

"I only answered his questions," I responded.

"Don't be smart with me. Get your sister and take her to the factory infirmary immediately," she shouted.

Realizing that the Hauptstrumfuhrer was helping me and knowing that there was no way that I could manage Joli by myself, I brazenly asked for help. Surprisingly, she agreed and assigned two girls and SS to accompany me to get Joli and take her to the factory hospital.

The Hauptstrumfuhrer and doctor were waiting for us. He checked Joli over and said that there was nothing that he could do for her. I began to cry, "You have to do something; she can't die. She has to live."

The doctor looked at the Hauptstrumfuhrer who then asked the doctor if there was anything at all that could be done. The doctor proceeded to say that the only thing he could try was to make an incision in Joli's side and to try and pull out some of the pus that was swelling her belly. He felt that her appendix had ruptured and that an infection had set in.

I told him to do it; however, he only proceeded when the Hauptstrumfuhrer ordered him to. He took a scalpel and made a small incision in Joli's side. He inserted a tube and yellow pus began to pour out of her. We watched as her belly shrunk back to its normal size. He stitched her up and covered the site with a bandage.

"Hauptstrumfuhrer, this is all I can do," the doctor said as he packed up his equipment and prepared to leave.

"You have to give her medicine so the infection doesn't come back," I begged.

He protested that he couldn't do that because he needed what little medicine he had to take care of the Russians and girls in forced labor. The Hauptstrumfuhrer ordered the doctor to give me the medication. The doctor gave me sixteen doses of a drug and told us to leave. I knew that he was afraid of what would happen to both himself and the Hauptstrumfuhrer if anyone found out what had been done.

After expressing my deepest gratitude, the girls and I took Joli back to our camp.

CHAPTER TWENTY-NINE

THE PLAN

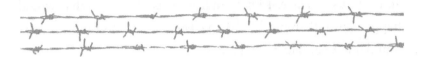

THE RUSSIAN PIPELINE HAD received information about the advancing Russian and Allied forces. Because Sasha's intelligence sources invariably proved reliable, I generally looked forward to his notes and whisperings. The Flossenburg concentration camp, just a few kilometers from us, was being liquidated. Prisoners were marched into the woods and shot. It was terrible to hear about the mass killings however, it meant the war was coming to an end; it also meant that the day of our possible murder was nearing.

In addition to Sasha's notes on the war, he frequently wrote of his love for me. He repeatedly told me he wanted to marry when the war was over. He was certain that I would love Moscow. He described his family in detail: they were intellectuals, studied law, very family oriented. He described his lifestyle, comfortable, by Soviet standards. He was certain that we would live happily ever after.

One day a note arrived at my station in its usual place beneath my machine. It described an escape plan that he and five other prisoners were working on. According to his note, I was to join him. I didn't answer him right away.

I gave a lot of thought to the seemingly madcap escape plan. On one hand, I worried about taking my chances waiting in the camp for liberation only to be gunned down in the end. However, there was equal chance of being gunned down during an escape. Even if we succeeded in escaping Hainichen, the Russians seemed to have no specific plans for afterwards. Would they meet up with some partisan groups operating in the woods and forested hills surrounding the camp? Would they attempt to make their way through the German defense lines to try and hook up with the approaching Russian forces? All of this was unclear.

Though on the surface the Russian plan seemed ludicrous to me, my state of mind was in such disarray that for a few moments I seriously considered the idea of escaping with Sasha. What brought me to my senses was that Joli was in no condition to come with us.

I responded to Sasha's proposal with a resounding *"no"* stating that I couldn't leave my ill sister. He in turn wrote me back telling me that he would come back to get me because he would not allow me to be shot like the other Flossenburg prisoners.

Sasha and I arranged to meet in a secure place between two fire doors. Friends on both sides would signal us if any guards approached. Our meeting was awkward. Sasha was still angry because I had said no to his escape plan. At first, we stood holding hands, his large blue eyes resting on me. He grabbed me and aggressively kissed me. I struggled to get myself free. He held onto me. I stopped resisting his kisses and kissed him back, passionately. Then I returned to my senses, and resisted again.

I would not be killed for a kiss. Even the Hauptstrumfuhrer would abandon me. I pushed Sasha away and demanded that he listen to me, "I cannot leave my sister. If you truly love me, you'll let me decide my own fate. If we both survive, we'll meet after the war. Escape if you must. Save your life."

"No," he said, "I love you and I won't leave you behind." He put his arms around me in an even tighter embrace. I heard his heartbeat against my ear.

"It is only terrible circumstances that have brought us together. Let's allow for a better time and place before we decide anything," I said. My words had a different effect on Sasha than what I had hoped for.

"Stop!" he said putting his hand over my mouth. "I will wait for the day the SS takes you to the Flossenburg forest where they shoot the Jews. I will rescue you there. Then you will know how much I love you."

His naively heroic and romantic imagination touched me, "Sasha, I know you love me. You already have proven it to me."

Sasha then started to talk about remaining at the factory so he could look after me. This news only made me more anxious. I did not want his death on my hands. Thousands of Russian prisoners had been routinely shot by the Nazis; who was to say that they would not be shot as the Allies approached.

"If you love me as much as you say you do, escape with your comrades, as soon as possible." My eyes filled with tears as I implored him to flee if he had the chance. I took his face in my hands and kissed both his cheeks and then his mouth. He no longer struggled against my wishes.

We embraced in silence. Our tryst was over.

CHAPTER THIRTY

THE FOREST

WHEN WE LEFT AUSCHWITZ in November of 1944, everyone thought that the German homeland was soon be overrun by the Americans, British or Russians. But that wasn't to be the case. We were still prisoners many months later, and with that the number of lives lost continued to rise from malnutrition and illness. It seemed everyone had some sort of chronic respiratory illness. The night air was filled with the sounds of coughing and hacking. Even so, things were not nearly as bad as they had been in Auschwitz.

On the last day of March, I was asleep in my bed when a terrific explosion woke me up. A second explosion caused panic and screaming amongst all the girls in the barrack. The roaring engines of military planes could be heard overhead. We were under attack. The SS came, shouting for us to get up and go downstairs. We were told that we were going to evacuate and march to another work camp. There was no need to dress as we always slept in our clothes. We grabbed our blankets and canteens and rushed out to the courtyard.

Once in the courtyard, I searched to see if the girls from the infirmary had made it out, but they were nowhere in sight. I had to find my sister so I made a mad dash to the infirmary. Joli and seven other girls were in their beds, panicking. A nurse had told them to get to their feet; only those that could walk would be included in the transfer. Joli was in no shape to walk to the courtyard let alone another camp. I told Joli to stay where she was and that I would be back for her. I left her in hysterics; she was terrified that I would leave her.

I dashed outside to find the Hauptstrumfuhrer. The day workers had been brought back from the factory. They had been moved to the underground bunker just in time; the factory had taken a direct hit and was now inoperable. We had all hoped for so long that the Russians would arrive and now I feared that their arrival would only be a means to our end.

Everyone was running around in confusion, even the SS. For a change, they made no threats to anyone. As I ran around looking for the Hauptstrumfuhrer, I saw girls loading food into a truck and onto a small wagon. *Ah Ha!* That gave me an idea about how I could transport Joli.

I ran to SS quarters and started screaming for the Hauptstrumfuhrer. He appeared on a balcony and told me to calm down. He asked me what I wanted. I tried and tried but I couldn't calm myself down. Through my heaving sobs I managed to tell him that I needed to save my sister. "Please get Joli on that truck," I pleaded, pointing towards the vehicle near the kitchen. He didn't respond. "I am NOT leaving Hainichen without her!"

"I can't manage it," he snapped at me. "The Lagerfurerin will be on her way to the infirmary to shoot the girls very soon. There is nothing I can do to stop the order." I was shocked that he didn't do anything to even try to mince his words to me.

The Hauptstrumfuhrer's words sent me into a rage. I could tell he was beyond caring, even about himself. At least he hadn't lied to me about the fate of the sick girls. I accepted him as a man who was essentially honest but dispirited and broken by the events taking place. I wondered if I could possibly convince him to get Joli on the truck and out of the camp. *What did I have to lose?*

I decided to go all out, heedless of the consequences. If he had lost his nerve, I would supply him with mine. "If you kill my sister, you will have to kill me first. You said you would save me, and now you are telling me that you are taking us into the Flossenburg forest to be shot. Are you getting ready to betray me?" I shouted.

"How do you know about that?" he asked in a way that revealed the truth of my comment.

"That doesn't matter. You said our fates are tied to one another's. What good would my death be to you?" I asked.

From the look on his face, I could see that my words were having the desired effect. I reminded him that he was supposed to be a *good* SS officer who might require the friendly testimony of a Jewish prisoner when the war was over. He sighed and shook his head.

"Bring your sister from the infirmary. Go quickly and do not let anyone see you. I will have her put on the truck and save both your lives, if possible."

I felt emboldened and asked about the other girls in the infirmary, "Please, there is no reason that the other girls in the infirmary need to die. There has been enough death. Can't you find it in your heart to save them, too?"

I apparently overdid it because he angrily responded, "No. Now go get your sister and get ready to march."

I ran as fast as I could into the infirmary. Joli was sitting on her bed crying.

"You are going to have to do your best to walk. Quickly. We need to go. Now!"

"Where are we going? What is happening? How am I going to go anywhere?" Joli asked, spattering out question after question.

"There is no time for questions. Just put as much of your weight on me and let's go now," I demanded.

I knew I wasn't supposed to bring the other girls but I couldn't leave them there to die.

"Everyone up!" I shouted. "The Lagerfuhrerin is on her way up to shoot everyone. Lean on each other and move out of here, NOW!"

The girls started to get out of bed and paired up to lean on each other.

"Follow me. Be quiet."

I took the majority of Joli's body weight onto myself and I helped her and all the rest of the girls out of the infirmary. We did it quickly and without being caught. The Hauptstrumfuhrer was waiting next to a truck for Joli and me.

"I arranged this truck for your sister," he said as we approached.

"And the other girls," I said, motioning to the other girls behind me. He must have been at a loss for words because all he did was nod as he held the door open for the girls to all climb in.

The sun was shining the day we marched out of Hainichen.

The smoke and dust were still heavy in the air although the bombardment had ceased. The air was thick and gritty. I could taste the war.

The streets were filled with civilians trying to evacuate the town. I was certain that they would not head in the direction of the approaching Russians, preferring whatever the Americans would dish out to the reputed vengeance of the Russians.

Joli and the other sick girls were safely in the truck at the rear of our line. I was worried about what the bumpy ride was doing to her weak and weary body however, I knew the bumps were better than whatever the miles and miles of walking would do to her.

The Hauptstrumfuhrer walked alongside our group, often keeping pace with me. We chatted back and forth in German. Both the SS and the girls wondered what was going on between us, thus I managed to project an air of distance and non-collaboration. But it was nice to have someone to talk to during the walk.

The Hauptstrumfuhrer had a sentimental streak; he told me that I reminded him of his daughter when she was my age. She was a school teacher and her husband was an SS Officer. He expressed hope that someone was helping her, wherever she was.

Before long, we arrived at an autobahn. It was multi-lanes and paved. I had never seen an autobahn. It was amazing to me to see such a road. Assorted military personnel, civilian, and other prisoner groups crowded the once vehicle traveled road. We were marched along the shoulder. Sasha was marching in a group on the other side of the road. Evidently, he had not tried to escape.

"Sasha!" I yelled out.

He threw a kiss in my direction as we passed each other. That was to be the last time I ever saw him.

The SS were everywhere and they were well armed. Guard dogs kept pace with us and growled fiercely whenever one of us veered from the line; two trucks full of soldiers rode at the rear of our group.

"Those are to be your executioners," the Hauptstrumfuhrer told me matter-of-factly.

Our formations grew longer and longer as more and more prisoners from other camps merged with us. Weariness caused some of the marchers to collapse; the Nazis shot them on the spot.

We had been marching for several hours without any water and hardly more than a few minutes rest. I don't know how many had collapsed or simply given up, but I regularly heard gunshots.

The sky was filled with the noise of cannon blasts as the German and Russian lines exchanged artillery fire. Planes flew overhead but none of them menaced the long lines marching alongside the autobahn. A new group of men and women caught up with us, another forced labor group, mostly Poles. They seemed to be healthy, maintaining a swift and steady pace while we wearily dragged ourselves along.

The Hauptstrumfuhrer had instructed me to move forward and walk at the front of my formation. He appeared periodically to give me the latest progress report. He told me that he would try and move our group towards the approaching Allies. If he couldn't manage to make that happen, he would have me instruct my group of girls to follow Russian prisoners when they turn away from Flossenburg.

Late in the afternoon, screaming sirens raced up from behind us. Two motorcycles and several cars passed us and stopped our groups' progress. The Russians prisoners were ordered to make an about face and march back, away from the direction of Flossenburg. Jewish marchers were ordered to continue ahead. The Hauptstrumfuhrer appeared alongside me and told me it was time to turn my group of girls around and to follow the Poles.

As I turned around with my small group of girls, other groups of prisoners were led towards the forest. We were now headed away from the Flossenburg forest. A great murmur of happy voices rose among us, especially those around me.

"Did my sister turn away from Flossenburg, too?" I asked the Hauptstrumfuhrer. I hadn't seen Joli during our march.

"She did," Hauptstrumfuhrer said, with a warm smile.

"Thank you, Hauptstrumfuhrer. Thank you with all my heart. You are a good man indeed. You not only saved me, but all of these girls," I said.

"It wasn't me, Edita, who saved these girls. It was you. If not for your endless persuasion, courage, and nagging I do believe the march would have continued on to the forest," the Hauptstrumfuhrer said to me.

"I don't believe that sir. I believe that in your heart you would have always done the right thing," I gave him a smile.

"You aren't done with your journey yet. The Americans are near. You will soon be free. But, first we have to get to a designated train station," he told me.

It was dusk when we arrived at the train station. The station house was severely damaged from an air raid. There were no longer benches or places to sit. Several took seats on the large pieces of debris or empty spots on the ground waiting for their next orders. The train was already nestled in waiting for us to load on as soon as the entire group marched its way into the station. When the truck that had carried Joli pulled up I ran to her and found her in bad shape. I helped her down from the truck. She could hardly walk.

We weren't at the station for long before the SS loaded a wagon with food and water. We were ordered into open coal cars. We had hardly settled in when the whistle sounded and the train moved ahead.

We were off again. For the next several days we shuttled back and forth. Planes flew overhead but none of them attacked the train tracks. As we passed through towns we heard sirens. On the third day we were handed a slice of bread. Joli spent most of the time asleep. I continued to feel her body to see if she was still alive. I was terrified that she wasn't going to survive the train ride. The coal cars had open doors so we were exposed to the elements. The weather was cold and rainy. We huddled together for warmth but it did little to keep us from being wet and miserable.

I wondered often what the Hauptstrumfuhrer meant when he said that we would be free "soon." I began to lose faith. Joli was failing. Her fever was so high. I didn't have anything if I didn't have Joli.

We began making frequent stops so we could relieve ourselves. Joli was not able to climb out of the coal car and I could not lift her out, nor could I get anyone to help me. I brought a bucket to the car so she could relieve herself. On these stops the German civilians taunted us; some threw stones.

We began to fight amongst ourselves. Fights occurred for more elbowroom; people stole from each other. Some just fought out of sheer frustration. Some girls went mad- some quietly, others loudly. Some died. Whenever we stopped, the bodies were lifted off the cars and left alongside the tracks. But no one attempted to escape, we were all too afraid of the Germans.

At one of the stops, I found the Hauptstrumfuhrer. As I approached him, I could see he looked troubled. His gray uniform was filthy and his overcoat hung over his drooped shoulders. I told him about Joli's condition, he told me that he was doing the best that he could. There was so much destruction everywhere.

"Do you know where we are going?" I asked.

"I am not sure," he answered, his voice ringing of desperation.

During that night, the train suddenly picked up speed, as though it had finally found its destination and was intent on getting there in the shortest time possible.

CHAPTER THIRTY-ONE

EN ROUTE

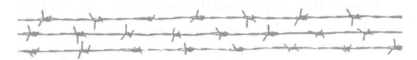

WE WERE TOSSED BACK AND FORTH and thrown into and on top of each other the rest of the route. I had Joli lie on top of me to ease the effects of the bumps and thumps on her damaged body. Finally, the train came to a halt. I rolled Joli off me and stood to see where we were. I heard cars being uncoupled. It wasn't long before the locomotive's whistle blew and the train started up again, leaving our uncoupled cars behind.

A short time later, the doors of our coal car opened and we tumbled out. An armed SS man told us we were free to roam alongside the river next to the tracks. We had stopped next to the Elbe River. The river serpentined to form a large looping half-circle around a field. We were ordered to remain inside the field. We were also told that if we heard sirens, we were immediately to get back into the coal cars.

We hadn't eaten anything for days. Many of the girls resorted to eating the grass and roots that grew along the riverbank. Having grown up on a farm, I knew what we could eat and what we couldn't. After looking around, I didn't see much we could. Joli and

I knew better, sometimes hunger outweighed the damage a bad weed could do to you so we waited for whatever scraps the SS may give us. We were finally given some food; most of which had rotted since we had gotten on the trains. As most starving people do, they ate what was provided. I picked away the rot and went with little in my belly. It was not long before most of the girls had taken ill, writhing in pain. It took a while for the immediate effects of the grass and roots to wear off and for stomachs to settle. Those of us who hadn't grazed or ate the rotting food were spared the ill effects.

We remained along the river for eight days. Fights broke out again. The Polish girls, who had stayed amongst themselves and not mingled with our group, began to harass us. The guards never interfered. Suddenly we heard sirens. We ran back into the coal cars as the airplanes above us prepared to drop their bombs. The planes fanned out of their formation. Seconds after we could hear loud explosions as bombs exploded on the towns and factories near us. The concussions from the bombs rocked the rail cars. The numerous explosions sounded like a rapid succession of thunderclaps. The bombings didn't last long.

The doors of the cars were reopened and once again we were told to get out. I went looking for the Hauptstrumfuhrer and found him standing by himself looking out towards the bombed city. He had tears in his eyes. Embarrassed, I turned to walk away. He stopped me and asked me what I wanted. I told him that if he truly cared about our welfare he would find shelter for us and get us some food. He replied that he had already sent a soldier ahead to look for shelter.

The next morning, I went looking for the Hauptstrumfuhrer again. When I found him, he was unshaven and looked even more depressed than the day before. He said he had good news and took me away from the cars to speak privately, "I have permission to march the Jewish girls to the nearest ghetto."

He went on to say that the Terezin ghetto was not a far walk and it was one of the *best*, a place for *privileged* German and Czech Jews. I knew something of this so-called model ghetto, for it was from this very one that thousands of *privileged* Jews had been shipped to Auschwitz: some into this model camp, others directly to the gas chambers. All of these *privileged* Jews were eventually were killed.

It seemed that our conditions had worsened and that we were further away from the American lines than ever. Despite this, I started to thank him for the efforts he had made to help me. He interrupted to tell me, once again, that I soon would be free and he would become a prisoner. He assured me that my sister and I would be safer in the ghetto than if he let us go free. He was certain if he freed us, the hostile German civilians would kill us.

Then he gave me alarming news. He said that it was impossible to take Joli to the ghetto because there was no way to transport her. The ill would be abandoned or shot where they lay.

"I am not leaving my sister behind, and neither are you! There is a wagon on the coal car that can be dragged to the ghetto."

The Hauptstrumfuhrer raised his hands above his arms like an angry father. He exploded, "You never give up!" He then lowered his voice and uttered, "I hope that my daughter has as much courage and will to survive as you do."

He looked off into the distance and said that his daughter was living in Dresden, which had been leveled by the previous day's bombings. He had no idea if she had survived or not.

The Hauptstrumfuhrer ultimately got the wagon unloaded from the train and had Joli and the other sick girls loaded onto it. I dared to think that the two of us might survive. It had been almost a year since our family had been taken and as far as I knew out of eleven there were only two left.

The Hauptstrumfuhrer ordered four girls to grab the tongue of the wagon and pull it, while SS guards marched alongside. The towns and villages we passed were lined with rubble. In places we had to weave our way around the debris. The buildings were still smoldering, dead civilians lay out along the road.

We passed through Litomerice and continued our way to Terezin. We arrived at the ghetto gate, tired and relieved. The Hauptstrumfuhrer stopped to converse with the guards. We were lined up and our names and numbers were recorded. The newly deceased were carried away. Though the German army was quickly falling apart, the SS maintained strict discipline. Six ghetto inmates, yellow Jewish stars wrapped around their arms, arrived to wheel or carry away the sick. An ambulance arrived to take Joli. I was told they were being taken to the ghetto hospital. The rest of us were ordered to sit on the sidewalk near the gate.

It was strange how my spirits rose and fell. I was relieved knowing that we were safer here than we had been in over a .year. I felt a sense of guilt for letting Joli go to the hospital alone, unable to protect herself.

My loss of Goldie wracked me with guilt. I kept reliving that last scene when that little girl trudged those final hundred yards to the gas chamber. Sometimes, on rare occasions, the memory of her courage boosted my own. But this day, sitting in front of the ghetto gates, depression overtook me and I was in danger of accepting the blackest of fates. Wallowing in self-pity, I heard my name being called, "Edita." I looked up and saw the Hauptstrumfuhrer standing over me with his hand outstretched.

"I have come to say good-bye and wish you luck, child," he said, his face warm and worn. I took his hand. He held my hand warmly in mine.

"I gave the hospital doctor instructions to take good care of Joli. You should have a good chance of surviving in the ghetto. The war will soon be over and you will be free again, just as I promised," he said.

"If you ever need me to testify to his kindness and lack of brutality, I will be available to help you," I said as I shook his hand.

As he walked off with the other SS officers, I saw him as an old and utterly broken man. I rued the times when my hatred of the SS uniform blinded me to his true nature, one of decency. It was he who, on his own authority, saved our little band of Jewish girls heading to death in the Flossenburg forest. It was he who had helped me keep Joli alive thus far. One hears stories of the *good* Germans, and there were many. But the *good* SS man or woman was rare indeed. Perhaps the number had grown in the last months of the war because they knew that their cause was doomed.

I never saw the Hauptstrumfuhrer again.

CHAPTER THIRTY-TWO

TEREZIN

THE TEREZIN GHETTO WAS LOCATED about ninety miles north of Prague. The site had impressive walls like a massive fortress, just like it was once. It was built by the Emperor Joseph II in 1780 and named for his Mother, the Empress Maria Theresa. Inside the gate were a number of two-story buildings as well as a number of very large barracks. It ceased to be used as a fortress in the late 19th century and languished until 1939 when the Nazis took over the western provinces of Bohemia and Moravia and made them a single German protectorate.

In the early war years, the Germans turned Terezin into a detention camp, a stopping place primarily for the Czech Jews on the way to Auschwitz. Thousands of Jews were packed together in extreme misery. These thousands were rapidly moved through to their annihilation. Toward the end of 1943, the SS transformed Terezin into a model ghetto, a camp that would promote the propaganda interests of the Nazi regime. Out came the tools to repair it: the cleaning supplies and the paint. Well-stocked shops appeared: a grocery, a bakery and a drug store were established. Even the surroundings were enhanced. The Nazis planted rosebushes and laid out lawns and strolling paths. The bandstand, park benches, children's playground and a café completed the picture. Inmates of the ghetto were advised on how to behave should important visitors come.

In June 1944, a visiting International Red Cross Commission arrived. The visit was a huge success for the Nazis. They brilliantly carried off their ruse. The Commission spent eight hours in Terezin and was shown only the newly repaired and painted buildings. They were allowed to speak to the ghetto Jews but only in the presence of the SS. The visiting Commission members never looked beneath the surface and behind the facades.

***

The guards led us through the gate and halted us in front of a huge brick building. We were taken inside to a room filled with bunks. They were set up in closely packed rows. Bread was distributed. I nibbled my small ration as a bird pecks its pellets. I laid down on a bunk and was joined by a bedmate. I was awakened during the night when my bedmate urinated in the bunk. She cried and apologized and explained that since she had arrived in Auschwitz she couldn't control her bladder. I decided sleeping on the floor was better than getting peed on. I had found an extra mattress to lie on so it wasn't too bad.

After a couple of weeks a few Polish girls took the mattress away from me. I ran out to the courtyard, my face buried in my hands, crying about the loss of my mattress.

"Why are you crying?" a man's voice asked me.

I raised my eyes expecting to see an SS, instead I saw a Jewish man, about thirty-years-old, wearing a yellow armband. He was a kapo who had authority over the courtyard. He introduced himself as Klein. When I told him what had happened, he said he would get me another mattress. Klein was as good as his word. I had my mattress, but, more importantly, he promised to help me locate my sister.

Klein was quick to arrange for me to see Joli at the hospital. He and his friend, Ludwig, risked their lives leading me upstairs, downstairs, over walls and past the patrolling SS guards. I found Joli among thirty other patients; she was as white as the sheet that was covering her. We had such a noisy reunion that some of the hospital staff came to investigate. One of the Hungarian doctors told me that Joli had been crying for me day and night. He introduced himself as Dr. David. I rose to shake his hand. When he touched my hand he asked for me to follow him. He led me into another room where he took my temperature.

"Your temperature is very high," Dr. David said, "I need to give you an examination. Is that alright with you?"

I nodded. I knew I hadn't been feeling well but I hadn't felt well in so many months that I wasn't sure if I was actually sick. My temperature was 103 degrees.

"Your lungs are very congested, probably from pleurisy," he said. I stayed quiet. I had no intention of being locked up in the hospital. "I urge you to get an x-ray and stay in the hospital," he continued.

"I am not going to stay in the hospital, Dr. David. I am sorry. I do appreciate your concern," I told him.

Dr. David tried to calm my fears but there was nothing he could do. Finally, he gave me a few pills and suggested an old-fashioned remedy to clear the mucous from my chest. I thanked him and promised to try his remedy.

Over the next few days, I managed with Klein and Ludwig's help to have regular visits with Joli. Ludwig worked in the kitchen. He gave me extra food for her. In addition, Klein sold some of the canned goods on the black market so I could get medication for Joli.

One day, when I was confined to my bunk with illness, Klein came to see me, bringing hot coffee and fresh bread. As I ate, he told me about his family. His Father was an important manufacturer in Berlin who had been sent to Dachau as a political prisoner. The rest of his family had been sent to Auschwitz. He announced that after the war we would get married and return to Berlin where he would restart his Father's business. I was shocked. An upper-class German Jew proposing to an eastern Jew. Rarely did this type of intermarriage occur. Flattered as I was, I turned down Klein's proposal as tactfully as I could. I gave him a long explanation that boiled down to the fact that I would never live in Germany. I also didn't know his real reason for proposing. Many marriage offers were thrown around in the camps. It wasn't about love in the camps. It was about the fear of loneliness, loss of family, the need to move on and I was still focused on finding my true love. Before long, Klein moved onto someone else determined to find a partner.

CHAPTER THIRTY-THREE

MAY 4, 1945

URING THE TWO MONTHS that we were in Terezin, the American troops advanced well into the heart of Germany and were liberating concentration camps and ghettos on their way. In Terezin, there was a hodgepodge of information ranging from vain imaginings, rumors, propaganda, and partisan intelligence.

The sounds of shelling grew louder each day. Long lines of German civilians, some wounded, left the area, dragging their few belongings behind them. The sight of Germans fleeing the Allies gave us joy. There were many young children and very old Germans among the refugees. I was thrown into a state of confusion as I watched one young German girl, about the same age as Goldie, trudge along. *Should I hate this little girl because she was from a nation that had murdered my Momma, sisters and brothers? How could I hate her?*

On the night of May 4th, a pain grabbed my lungs and wouldn't let go. I took the medicine that Dr. David had given me; it dulled the agony so that I was able to fall into a restless sleep. Shortly into my hazy rest I was awakened by shouting and singing. I got up, rubbed the fog from my eyes and went to the window. The moon lit up the courtyard below, I was able to see prisoners dancing and frolicking in the streets. People were shouting, "We are free! We are free!" Other prisoners were working to loosen the stones that formed the enclosing wall. There was not a single SS in sight.

Some of the other girls started to stir. I began to shout, "We are free! We are free!" I completely forgot about my pain. Great excitement broke out. Everyone went about congratulating one another for making it through the war. Tears of happiness began to fall from my eyes as I shouted again, "We are free!"

A new craziness began to erupt. We ran out of the barracks and into the ghetto streets to mix with those who had already started celebrating. Everyone was screaming insanely. Weak as we were, there was no denying us our day of happiness and relief. Delirious ecstasy took over Terezin and nothing could stop it.

The celebrators broke out of the ghetto seeking plunder in the nearby community of Litomerice. Food was the main booty, but weapons and luxuries like clothing and jewelry were high on the list. Some of the men who had managed to get hold of rifles and small arms were exuberantly shooting them in the air. Liberating Russians were few and far between so we enjoyed the anarchy of the hour before the main force could lay down their occupation laws.

I followed along with the crowd, pumped with the excitement at the prospect of getting my share. By the time I reached the town, every store had been broken into. The storeowners foolish enough to stand watch over their property were either beaten or shot. The rampaging Jews put their booty into cartons and headed back to Terezin.

My mind was set on finding a bakery to obtain bread and sweets to fill up Joli's stomach and mine. Apparently the bakers had only recently fled because the bread was still warm in the first bakery I found. What a happy sight; what a delicious smell. I grabbed a loaf and kissed it; then I broke off a little piece and swallowed it. The sweet soft dough was so satisfying. I chewed slowly to savor the taste. I took a small flour sack and placed three loaves of bread in it. I left the bakery to look for a butcher shop. I wanted to find smoked ham for Joli. The doctor had told me that protein would be good for her. I found a butcher shop full of meats. It had already been ransacked yet I was able to find a salami and a ham. I took a bite out of the salami. My mouth watered. I was so excited to take my findings back to Joli.

On my way back to Terezin, a column of Russian troops were making their way down the road. I ducked into a corridor until they passed. Although the Russians were our liberators, they had a reputation for plunder and rape. I had plenty reason to fear them.

We spent much of the night talking about what we would do after our release. For most of us, returning to our hometown was out of the question. Our homes were gone. Most of our families were gone. Most of our neighbors had cooperated in and gladly received or seized our belongings and property. As much as we were overtaken with relief we were filled with fear over our futures.

I was sick; I was young – just eighteen. When I could push the grief I felt aside, I was hopeful. I hoped that with the return of my health, I might salvage something of a life. Yet, I knew that the legacy of the camps and ghettos would always remain in my mind and heart.

But, in those early days of post-liberation, I had more immediate concerns. First and foremost was my deteriorating health. It seemed that while I had survived Hitler's war against the Jews, I was in danger of succumbing to the aftereffects. Then there was Joli to worry about; she was in far worse condition than I was.

CHAPTER THIRTY- FOUR

A NEW FEAR

MY CONDITION WORSENED to the point that I could barely move. Emotionally, I deteriorated, too. I had long crying fits and felt tremendous guilt over some of the things I had done, had not done and should have done those during my days in Auschwitz II- Birkenau, Hainichen and Terezin.

While I no longer faced murder by the Nazis, I was in danger of being done in by my pleurisy or some other ailment. My ribs protruded out of my torso. My extremities were swollen from malnutrition. My labored breathing was taking everything out of my tiny body. I was so wrought up and filled with worry and agitation that sleep became impossible. But then again, sleep brought horrifying dreams and nightmares that tore at my core. My usual resolve and inner sources for fighting adversity had deserted me. My loss of will began to frighten me as I started accepting the notion of my death. My concern for Joli intensified. *Had I done the right thing by keeping Joli from volunteering for work details; would she be sick now?* My deep despair at the loss of Goldie had returned with such force that it almost overwhelmed me. *Had I done the right thing by ever stealing Goldie away from the gas chambers and making her suffer for six months?* Had I been right to fight so hard for Joli and me as now it appeared that both she and I would die in these hours of liberation? *Such irony.* God seemed to still be playing a cruel trick. Facing me was a lonely death in a ghetto barrack without a loved one or a friend to hold my hand.

There was no one to talk to. Every survivor in Terezin was suffering their own tragedies and uncertainties; everyone had their own demons to face.

A few days later, I was feeling little stronger. The beautiful spring day helped with my spirits. From my second story window, I could see a long caravan of Soviet tanks, wheeling in cannons and trucks loaded with soldiers, a long column of marching foot soldiers followed behind. Most of the liberated Jews felt as I did: the Soviets had purposely held their troops back from taking Auschwitz so the Nazis would have more time to finish off the Jews. Right or wrong, this was the way we felt. It was by chance that the Russians had liberated us from Terezin; it had not been a rescue mission.

There was a lot of frenzied activity in the courtyard; people were running about. Russian nationals spaced themselves out to be ready for a return trip to their homeland. The rest of the nationalities were to be processed through Prague. The sick were ordered to line up at a table near the entrance of a field hospital where a large canvas tent had been erected.

I was supposed to register with the Russians per a plan, based on geography, devised by the Allies and Russians. I didn't want to register with the Russians; deep in my heart I felt that this was wrong for me. I also feared that, given my physical state, I would be sent to the hospital where unhygienic conditions would surely kill me.

I refused to report to the field hospital where complete chaos reigned. Thousands reported being ill. The sick and dying were all thrown together, no matter the illness: typhus, dysentery, scarlet fever, tuberculosis. I decided to take my chances elsewhere. The streets of Terezin were crowded with thousands of people. Even though the Star of David was no longer ordered to be worn, it was still obvious which persons were Jews; the marks of the camps worn in their physical appearance. It looked as if a strong wind would knock down their skeletal frames.

Freedom had its hazards and ironies. The starving, walking freed Mussulmen couldn't digest the volumes of rich foods they had gorged on; many died from gluttony. Those too weak or disabled to get at the looted food were spared.

I finally found enough energy and went in search of my sister. Tired, I stopped to rest in a park. My mind slipped off into thoughts of the past and future. Once upon a time, I would have been so happy in this park: the flowers, the budding trees. Had the *Nazis stolen my happiness? Was I going to let them do that to me? Was that not the same as letting them kill me?* In this reverie, I did not hear the approaching steps of a Soviet soldier until he stood in front of me. I started to move away but he caught my hand. I screamed at him in Russian, "Leave me alone!"

"Shhh, I am not going to hurt you. I heard you crying. I am just stopping to check on you. Is there something I can do to help?" he asked.

Something about him reminded me of Sasha. I decided to ask him about Sasha, perhaps he could help me find him.

"I don't know this Sasha you speak of. But Miss, you should stay out of the park and off the streets if you can. Some of my comrades often get drunk and are very sex-starved. They tend to not behave in the nicest of ways."

"Thank you for the warning," I said.

I waited for the solider to leave the park and I left shortly after. I walked to the ghetto hospital. When I found Joli she was crying. I had not seen her for two days. I ran towards her and threw my arms around her.

"I thought you were dead!" she yelled.

"Well, you can see I'm not," I said, trying to make her smile.

"You look sick," she said to me.

"I am fine," I told her trying to assure her that nothing was wrong.

I proceeded to break out the bread and smoked ham I had looted earlier. Dr. David saw that I was back at the hospital and came over to check on me. He touched my forehead and immediately ordered an examination. In didn't take but a matter of minutes to confirm that my pleurisy had worsened and that I had also contracted pneumonia. Dr. David instructed me how to take care of myself in the barracks, knowing full well that I would not enter the hospital.

Back at the barracks, some of the girls worried about catching my illnesses. They were making such a fuss that I was afraid that they would forcibly carry me off to the hospital. I told them that I would sleep facing away from them and cover my mouth when I coughed. They finally agreed to let me stay.

During the night the barracks erupted with terrible screams. Russian soldiers had entered our sleeping quarters. They were drunk and yelling: "You gave yourselves to the Germans but not us, you whores." One of the Russians threw a girl down and was immediately on top of her, tearing her clothes off, raping her. The terrified screams continued.

I pulled my blanket over my head, hoping to hide on the mattress on the floor. Suddenly my blanket was yanked back and a soldier stood, lustfully surveying my body. I was wearing handmade panties and a wet towel that I had wrapped around my chest as Dr. David had advised. The soldier was tall and I could smell the alcohol that wafted off of him. Apparently deciding I was the one for him, he threw his coat and hat onto the floor. I quickly stood up and as I did the towel fell off me exposing my bare breasts. I tried to retrieve it but the soldier snatched it and laughed loudly. I backed against the wall, hugging my chest in an attempt to hide my bare breasts.

"Please, leave me alone. I never gave myself to a Nazi or any other man! Please!" I begged.

My pleas seemed to amuse him and made him laugh again, "A virgin. You'll be a special treat for me." My attacker unbuttoned his pants with one hand while he held me against the wall with the other. I screamed and tried to push his huge hand off of me.

Once he had unbuttoned his pants, he freed his other hand. Both of his hands were pushing against my breasts. The pressure on my weakened lungs sent sharp pains through my chest. I flailed at him, fighting him with every ounce of energy that I had in my body.

I scratched his face: "You will have to kill me before you will rape me!" I shouted. I was kicking and throwing my arms at his face as hard and fast as I could.

He grew angry and slapped me across the face. I fell to the floor. He pulled his gun out of its holster. He dropped to the ground and straddled me. He put his gun to my temple. His face was an inch from mine, he forced his foul smelling mouth against mine. He was going to rape me or kill me or both.

"If you don't get up and out of here, I will blow your brains out," a voice said in Russian. The men in the barrack started retreating. My eyes were closed so tight. I waited until the pounding of the boots silenced before I opened my eyes again.

When I opened my eyes, the lights were on and a Russian officer stood holding a pistol against the head of my attacker. It was the Russian officer who I had met in the park. A few of the girls from the barrack were able to get out and ran for help and luckily someone was actually willing to help. I was saved.

***

So this was liberation? Every night thereafter we barred the doors. Even in the daylight the ghetto was not safe. Girls were attacked and raped, sometimes their boyfriends forced to look on helplessly. Things deteriorated; it became imperative to get out of the ghetto.

I clung to the great hope of a reunion with someone from my family. As I walked the streets to see Joli, I searched for faces I might recognize. I hoped that somehow someone from my family would be alive and would find me.

CHAPTER THIRTY- FIVE

REUNION

ORCI, MY ELDEST BROTHER, had survived the war. He traveled to Prague to search for survivors of our family. He set out by checking the lists of people that had registered on the survivor lists, something that I hadn't done. One day a man overheard Morci describe me to a group of people. The man approached my brother.

"Did you say Kalus?" the man asked my brother.

"I did. My sister's names are Sura Rifka, Joli and Goldie Kalus. Have you heard if they are alive?" Morci asked the man.

"I don't know a Sura Rifka but I worked with a girl in the Hainichen factory named Edita Kalus."

Morci had no way of knowing I had abandoned my given name, Sura Rifka, and adopted the name of Edita. He would have thought the man was talking about someone from another family, but the man went on to describe Edita Kalus and Morci thought that Edita sounded very similar to Sura Rifka and decided to make the trip to Terezin to find this Edita Kalus, just in case.

Be it luck or fate, but things always seemed to have a funny way of working themselves out, because it just so happened that on one of the days that I was combing the streets for family and there was Morci, looking for me. We had found each other!

A flood of relief overcame me. My eyes began to fill with tears. I couldn't hold them back. Before I could even reach him to wrap my arms around him the tears erupted over my eyelids and poured down my face.

"What is with the name change, Edita?" he said, dragging out my new name.

Laughter broke through my tears. I told him about the name change and that Goldie didn't make it and Joli did. He said he didn't know about my brothers or Papa. But, we didn't discuss more than that. It was too raw for both of us. We knew we had survived and in that moment that was all we needed to know.

Morci had a plan for the future. That was more than I had. He was going to take me and Joli back to Prague. I was willing to go anywhere and glad Morci had somewhere to go. But the first destination was to see Joli in the hospital, so that is where we went.

Because Joli and I had not registered we didn't have any papers. And, Joli wasn't in the condition to be transported without an ambulance. Morci contacted a friend of his and explained our situation. His friend, Itzu, had served on a labor camp work force that had dug trenches and bunkers for the Germans. After some time, the Russians captured the work force and allowed him to 'volunteer' in the Czech Brigade that was fighting against the Nazis. Itzu managed to contact a magistrate and arrange for papers for Joli and me. He also arranged for an ambulance to take Joli to a hospital in Prague. Itzu promised to arrange for both Joli and I to get into a sanatorium to heal.

With my meager belongings, my hand-sewn underwear and dress, Sasha's letters, and two small pins Sasha had made for me packed in a small suitcase we prepared to leave. We got Joli situated on the ambulance and then headed to the train station.

When we arrived at the train station in Prague, Morci ran into an old girlfriend. The two of them began talking. I walked away to give them some space. While I was waiting for Morci to finish up someone came running up to me at full speed. Before I could jump out of the way the man knocked me to the ground, my suitcase flew out of my hands, the man grabbed it and ran off.

"Hey!" I yelled, coughing. As I pushed myself back onto my feet, I started looking for my suitcase. It was gone. The man had stolen my bag. I began to cry.

A young Russian officer approached me and asked why I was crying.

"My suitcase was stolen. Those were all the belongings I had," I told him.

"Don't you worry. I can help you replace everything you lost. Follow me," he said.

The young officer took me into a large room in the station house. Lined along one wall were German men and women, some handcuffed, others with their hands held behind their heads. Stacked against the other wall was a collection of suitcases.

"Help yourself," the officer said pointing to the pile. "You may also look over these people to see if any of them were the ones who tortured you in the camps; you can take your revenge."

Many of the detained men and women showed evidence of being beaten. I searched for the Hauptstrumfuhrer and SS Officer Dali. I wanted to vouch for their kindness. While looking over the line, the officer told me that the captives had been lucky to escape revenge shootings by other soldiers and ex-prisoners. I couldn't bear to be in the room one minute more. I had enough brutality, even against the SS. I ran back to my brother, without a suitcase.

***

"Here we are," Morci said, as he opened the door to the hotel room he had in Prague. The room was small but it was ours, and just ours. There was one bed and a couch. Best of all there was a tub. I soaked in that tub for hours. I prayed that the warm water would wash away the memories of the past.

In the morning, Itzu came. It was through him that I was able to get a bed in the Podolski Sanatorium. I agreed to enter a hospital because I knew that I could not shake my illness on my own. Morci's daily visits were the highlight of my day. Often he brought along a friend with whom he had reunited.

A marriage epidemic took place among the concentration camp survivors. Following the personal catastrophes of the war, there was an urge to establish new roots and a new family. Middle-aged survivors seemed in the greatest hurry to replace lost spouses and children. Numerous offers of marriage came my way, one of which was from Itzu.

But, despite Itzu's kindness, on the matter of marriage, I was still determined to marry for love. This ruled out marriage for reasons of convenience. As I lay in bed, I often thought of the pure, lost love Jacob and I had shared back home. The memory of that love helped insulate me from easily accepting another man, however kind.

One day, I set out for Joli's hospital where she was scheduled to have her kidney removed; I had promised to be there. As I walked to the streetcar, a car's horn blew and stopped by me. Itzu was in the car, driven by a man I had not seen before. Itzu had brought his friend Sol, someone he knew from his work force and had worked with on the Czech Brigade. Apparently, Itzu brought Sol along so he could show off his young virgin, blonde hair, blue-eyed, future bride. When Sol asked how Itzu knew I was a virgin, Itzu responded that he had asked my brother. Being a virgin in these days was highly prized. Most men assumed that women who had survived Auschwitz had done so by trading sex for food.

I reacted poorly to Itzu's comments and to his companions spectating: "Do I pass inspection? What gives you the right to judge me? Not every girl sold herself for food or clothing." Before anyone could answer, I lectured both on how a woman should be treated. I told them I didn't like feeling as though I was standing for inspection in front of the SS guard. I reminded them that their own experiences as prisoners should have made them more respectful of concentration survivors.

Sol looked away from me, ashamed. Finally, there came an apology and an admission that he believed the worst about female survivors. Sol had an embarrassed look on his face. To escape a further lecture, he asked Itzu to drive me to the hospital alone. On the drive, Itzu proceeded to describe the life he and I would have: travel through Europe and immigrate to Israel where we would raise a family. I questioned him as to how he had come up with this plan and who had given him permission to make such plans; he responded "Morci."

"Itzu, I am in charge of myself and I will would make my own decisions," I told him.

I stayed with Joli until she woke from her surgery but I needed to return to the sanatorium before dinner. Morci came to see me and we had quite the discussion about Itzu.

"If you love Itzu so much, you marry him!" I told Morci.

He laughed at me. "Always wanting to do your own thing, Rif...I mean Edita." His smile didn't fade. "I have good news."

"What? Tell me!" I said, quickly dropping our argument.

"Papa is alive!"

I could hardly breathe and this time it wasn't from the pleurisy, it was from happiness, "Are you sure? How do you know?"

"I got word from a friend that Papa had gone back to our hometown to see if he could get any of our property back."

A week later, I went to the YMCA where Morci was waiting for me. Inside, stood Morci with Papa. I exploded into his arms. He told me that my brothers Moshe and Labji were also alive and we would see them soon. In the meantime, I had my Papa all to myself. He told me of others. I learned that Jacob had gotten ill and was sent from the work camp to Auschwitz. Papa said he didn't know if Jacob survived. I cried. I had loved him so much. I had thought that if I was strong enough to make it that Jacob would have also survived.

After I described my experiences to Papa, I listened to his story of Buchenwald where he and my brothers had worked in a stone quarry breaking and cutting stone. The strict production quota kept them working long hard days. As in every other Nazi workplace, those who failed to fill quotas were put to death. My Papa sometimes had trouble meeting his quota and was on occasion taken out of the group, destined for death. My brothers were able to persuade an SS guard to allow them to make up for any of Papa's shortfall.

Sometime later, they were transported to a factory that produced gasoline out of coal. The factory was a constant target for Allied bombers. During these bombardments, the Germans forced the Jewish slaves to stand in the courtyard of the factory. The Germans reasoned that if the reconnaissance aircraft saw prisoners they might ward off further air attacks. If not, the Jews would die in the raids. The tactic did not work. The Allies chose to bomb the cities nearby instead of the factory. Following the raids, the SS would round up the Jews and execute them. As they were being led to the killing forest, a Lagerfuhrer who seemed to like Moshe told them he wouldn't notice if he and nine other men attempted to escape.

My Papa and brothers made their escape but Moshe was brought down by a pursuing German shepherd and wound up in front of the Lagerfuhrer. My Papa and the others had hidden in barns during the day and traveled at night searching for the Americans who were in the area. During the first night of their escape the owner of the barn discovered them. Instead of turning them over to the SS, he helped them move to a safer place where they were provided with food and a change of clothes.

Once more, the Lagerfuhrer helped Moshe escape; this time he was successful, having come upon a band of partisans. Later,

Moshe recognized the Lagerfuhrer among the captured SS and was happy to testify as to his kindness and to sign papers that exonerated the man from the worst crimes. With the war coming to an end, SS officers and guards were more than willing to perform good deeds in hope that the actions would later save their lives.

Papa had gone back to our hometown of Vlachovice, which was now annexed by the Russians. There he found the two post-cards I had been required to mail from Auschwitz carrying the message that all was well and we were happy. Our property had been distributed to neighbors who had been told we were dead. The Russians had confiscated the family's mill and the house had become the property of the town. No one offered to return anything to us. In fact, when Papa went to the Mayor to try to get back our horse back or to gain possession of the filly the horse had birthed he pulled out a rifle and threatened to kill my Papa. He left Vlachovice empty handed.

Papa discovered that our family had more surviving members than any of the other families in town: six of the eleven of our family members were alive at the end of the war.

In time, I was reunited with all three of my brothers and we were all reunited with Joli who was still in poor condition but out of the hospital and on the mend.

CHAPTER THIRTY-SIX

SOL

WHEN I LEFT THE YMCA that day I was surprised to find Sol waiting in his car for me without Itzu. He offered to drive me back to the Podolski Sanatorium but I wanted to be alone with my thoughts.

"Please. I owe you an apology for earlier. I feel terrible. Let me try to make it up to you," he said.

I accepted his offer and climbed into the car. On the drive, he seemed different from how I had perceived him to be on our earlier meeting. He was kind, charming, and funny. Sol's old tan car pulled into the sanatorium. I was glad I had accepted the ride. It felt nice to feel like a normal girl, even though I was being dropped off at a hospital.

"Thank you for the ride, kind sir," I said with a grin.

"You are welcome, fair lady," he said smiling back.

He was so handsome. I stared into his dark black eyes and started to lose myself for a moment. "Well then, this is good-night," I said, reaching for the door.

"Edita, would it be okay if I were to visit you and to drive you between the sanatorium, and Joli's hospital and the YMCA where your family is staying while I am on furlough?" he asked.

"I would appreciate that."

"It would be my pleasure. I will pick you up at 10 am tomorrow," he said, his smile wide.

Sol's increasing interest provoked my Papa to ask him of his intentions. The cross examination embarrassed Sol because he knew how my Papa felt of Itzu; he had a good education and excellent prospects (monies buried before the family was taken away). Sol knew that my Papa felt that Itzu was a better match for his daughter, and that Itzu was planning on proposing to me. Even so, Sol kept his pursuit. As my ride, Sol joined us at most family dinners, and at most dinners, my Papa would remind Sol over and over that I deserved better. And like most nights, back at the sanatorium, I had to apologize for my Papa.

"I don't mind. I respect your Father's concerns," he said.

"Either way, he doesn't have to be rude. You are so sweet to me," I said, blushing.

My roommate took a moment to chime in, "Don't be shy, Sol, kiss her good-bye," she said giggling.

Both Sol and I turned red, but Sol decided to ask, "Would you be willing to accept a kiss from me, Edita?"

"How can I refuse someone as nice as you?" I said. He took my face in the palms of his hands and kissed me gently on the lips, not passionately, very gently. I couldn't help but feel I was falling in love with him.

He smiled at me, "Sleep well, sweet Edita," he said, and left the room.

★ ★ ★

The next morning Sol arrived with a large new suitcase. "It's a surprise. Open it," he said. The suitcase contained underwear, blouses, dresses, skirts and medicine that he had bought on the black market. I was so excited. I couldn't help but smile, fully. Sol enjoyed my appreciation of the wholly unexpected largess.

He turned to me and said, "This is my way of showing how much I care about you."

As excited as I was, I had to hold back, "I'm sorry, I can't accept your generous gift."

He was ready for this response. "Too bad," he said, a smile forming across his face, "nothing can be returned. You have to accept them. I have no one else to give them to."

I looked down at the beautiful things in the suitcase. I really wanted to keep them. I hadn't had any clean clothes in so long. However, I was used to everything coming with a price. Before I could say anything, Sol spoke, "The only string attached to the gifts is that I am allowed to visit you again. Does that sound fair?" Sol asked.

I blushed and smiled and turned bright red.

"I will take that as a yes," Sol said, leaning in for another gentle kiss.

Gradually, Sol's personality, gentleness, and love helped me to open my heart to him; soon I could not think of another man. But my Papa and brothers still preferred Itzu and couldn't understand why I didn't feel the same way.

Sol and his love became more and more important to me. I decided to talk with my Papa. I told him that my experiences in the camps had made me very independent and quite able to decide things for myself. My assertiveness was a hard thing for him to swallow. Traditionally, parents had a large say in choosing their children's spouses, especially their daughters. But the war had changed the world as we had known it.

The night I had my discussion with my Papa, the Sanatorium announced plans to transfer the respiratory patients, which included me, to a hospital just outside of Prague. Sol, upon hearing this, suggested that I sign out into his care and come live with his aunt and uncle in Prague. My Papa, equal to the challenge, insisted that I leave with him and go to Budapest, check into a hospital there, and live with his sister in the city. Sol begged me to go with him. He tried to convince me that my Papa only wanted to separate us.

It was a difficult choice, but in the face of my quandary and uncertainty, my Papa's wishes prevailed. Sol and I had a sorrowful parting as I boarded a train to Budapest. It was hard leaving Sol and Joli, who was still in the hospital.

"I will return to you when I am well. We will be together soon," I told him, my hands clutching his. The only solace I had in the moment was that I knew that I would actually be able to reunite with Sol, if he would take me back, after I left him. Sol's furlough was over the following week and he would be returning to duty.

"Please be careful. There have been several attacks on the trains," was all he said before he left.

***

The destruction and ruin across the towns was catastrophic. But inside the train, people were happy, many were singing in their various languages. I was enjoying the sunshine on my face and the simple chit-chat with Morci and my Papa. For the first time in years we all had hope.

The train had traveled about 50 kilometers from Prague when a tall, husky Russian soldier came up to me and demanded that I get up so that he could sit down and have me sit on his lap. His breath reeked of alcohol. At first I pretended not to understand him thinking that perhaps he would go away. That didn't work. The Russian made sure his intentions were clear when he pulled out his gun. My Papa and Morci were pleading with the soldier. My heart was pounding. *Did we all really get this far to end up here, staring down the end of a Russian soldier's gun, again?* Suddenly, out of nowhere, Sol appeared. He pulled out a gun and pointed it at the Russian's head.

"You wouldn't hurt a woman who belongs to a man who fought alongside you, would you?" he challenged.

I wasn't certain if it was Sol's appeal to a soldier's sense of camaraderie or the gun to his head that convinced the Russian to apologize and leave the car but whatever the case, Sol's utterly unexpected appearance needed explanation.

Sol sat down across from us, "I don't intend to live without you, Edita."

Sol was determined and was not to be stopped by anyone, including my Papa or his furlough ending. Sol's words stunned my

Papa into a silence that was not to be broken until we reached Budapest. My brother simply watched with amusement and admiration for Sol's resolve to have his way. What could they say or do in the face of an ardent suitor who would brook no interference? My Papa struggled to accept the inevitable: that this bold young soldier had thrust himself dramatically into his daughter's heart.

My Papa's sister, Aunt Millie, Moshe and Lajbi met us at the train station in Budapest. Sol and I were pleased when my Papa introduced Sol as my fiancée. He asked Aunt Millie if she would make the arrangements for our wedding. We were to be married two days later.

CHAPTER THIRTY-SEVEN

FOR BETTER OR WORSE

ULY 28, 1945 WAS A BRIGHT DAY in Budapest. It was the
day Sol and I were to be married, six weeks after our
initial meeting. It was a humble ceremony, to say the
least. Sol wore a borrowed suit that was two sizes too large. My
borrowed wedding dress was even larger. The ceremony was
held in a kosher Jewish restaurant. We had to invite strangers
from the restaurant to fill out the minion (quorum) of ten males
required for our marriage prayers.

Attending was my Papa, my three brothers, my aunt and uncle, their daughter and two friends from Chynadiyovo. Tears of
joy flowed intermittently with our tears of sorrow for our family
members that didn't survive the Holocaust. As the Rabbi intoned
the prescribed Orthodox rite, I thought of Momma's promise
that could not be kept: *Rifchu, I will make you a wedding this
town will never forget.* How I missed my Momma on my wedding
day. But I knew I was only here because of her, I had survived
because of the promise I had made to my Momma.

A few days later Sol and I had to head back to Liberec where
he was stationed for duty. Liberec was only a one-hour drive from

Prague. Joli was still in the hospital thus I was very happy to be returning that way where I knew I could keep an eye on her.

Sol had a hotel room in Liberec. It was small but clean and a place to call our own. It was a blissful time except for the many nights that were interrupted by my horrible dreams and nightmares, a legacy of the death camp. Sol was tender and comforting in his attention to my almost nightly cries. When I woke up screaming, his love flowed into my heart and dissipated my fears.

Following Sol's discharge from the army we were given a four-bedroom house, a reward from the Czech government for Sol's record of bravery in the army. Along with the house, Sol was given the proprietorship of a coal supply company in Lobendava, where we would later move.

My horror filled nights continued. We thought a change of scenery could help. We thought by fulfilling my dreams of heading to America the nightmares would end. Our names were one of five hundred listed on the emigration quota for the United States, but the emigration numbers moved very slowly.

Meanwhile, Joli had been getting healthier by the day while living with my Papa. My brothers were making reasonably good adjustments as well. In 1947, Joli, always the restless one, got married and packed up and left for Palestine to join the independence movement that was taking place.

One February 7, 1948, I gave birth to a daughter we named Shoshana. Our joy was complete for the moment. However, there was political unrest in Czechoslovakia. The Communists overthrew the democratic Czech government, the borders were closed and no further emigration was permitted. Sol had refused an offer to become mayor of Lobendava, because of this he was suspected of having anti-Communist sympathies. This put him in imminent danger of arrest. We received a tip from a friend in the police department that Sol was to be arrested in the coming weeks. Sol decided to leave for Prague in hopes of devising a plan for us to leave Czechoslovakia.

***

"We will be together soon," Sol said, as he was getting ready to leave for Prague. I knew that the only way this would be true is if he could get out of the city and to Prague. However, it always seemed like something was tearing me away from the people I loved.

I tried not to cry as Sol left Shoshana and me behind. I knew he needed me to be strong, but I was tired, tired of having to be strong all the time. I kissed Sol good-bye, "Be careful. We love you," I told him.

The same night that Sol left for Prague, the KGB and police came knocking at my door in search of him.

"Where is he, Mrs. Perl?" they asked, staring me down, trying to scare me. What they didn't realize was that I had been threatened by far worse than them. I looked them straight in the eye and told them he was working in the coal mines and I didn't know when he was returning home.

"I will be sure to have him report to the police station as soon as he gets home," I said sweetly.

"Make sure you do that, Mrs. Perl. If he doesn't return soon, we will be back."

Once again, my family was being threatened. Once again, I had to make a major decision to avoid a potentially mortal threat. I began to cry. *Was there ever going to be peace in my life?*

Pull it together, Edita! I wiped my tears away and puffed up my chest. I dressed my seven-month-old baby and packed some things in a large handbag. In the early morning, I slipped out of the house and into the garage where our Opal Blitz was parked. I hid our legal papers and a small amount of money in the spare tire. Two hours later I locked the house, placed the baby on the back seat of the car, turned over the motor and began another new journey.

I had to stop by Moshe's house before I could leave town. I couldn't leave my family wondering what had happened to Shoshana and me. When Moshe opened the door he could tell something was wrong before I even said anything.

"What can I do to help, Edita?" he asked.

"Nothing," I said, holding back my tears, "I came to let you know I'm leaving. I don't know where I am going. And, I don't know where Sol is," I said.

Moshe interrupted me, "You really don't know where he is?"

"I really don't know where he is. That is the safest thing. And, the safest thing is for you not to know where I am going," I told him.

"Edita, I think I can handle myself."

"After everything Moshe, we don't need to find out. I will call you and let you know I am safe as soon as I can. I will let you know where I am once I know that everyone is safe from the KGB," I told him.

We hugged each other and I left. I could have driven straight to Prague from Lobendava but I was worried that the KGB may be following me so I decided that a direct route wasn't an option. I decided to drive to the next town. I wasn't sure what I was going to do. I needed gas and knew I had to pull off at the next service station. I thought that this is where I could possibly make my next move. Instead of getting gas, I took Shoshana into the store to talk to the store manager.

"Excuse me, sir?" I asked the man behind the counter.

"Yes, ma'am," he replied.

"Do you see that grey Opal out there?" I asked.

He nodded.

"Would you be interested in buying it? I will take whatever you are willing to give me."

He came out from behind his desk and walked out to the car. He didn't say much as he walked around the car.

"Will you buy the car?" I asked.

He nodded again.

I packed up my belongings from the car and asked the man to drive me to the train station. I boarded the train to Prague, holding Shoshana tight to my chest. While the accommodations on this train were worlds apart from the train ride to Auschwitz, I was equally as scared. I arrived in Prague and made my way to Sol's Aunt Udel's house. The police had lost track of us. For three weeks, I anxiously awaited word from Sol.

★★★

I finally heard from Sol. When he had arrived in Prague, he had encountered a group of men speaking Hebrew. They had told him of a group, the Haganah, which was recruiting people to fight in Palestine for a Jewish homeland. He was immediately accepted and sent to a training camp, which was sponsored by, of all people, the Russians.

We were told to stay where we were and he would give notice as to when we would be brought to his base and then begin our journey to Palestine. We waited and waited. Two weeks passed when there was a knock on the door. A young man in a uniform stood before me, "Mrs. Perl?"

"Yes?" I asked, hesitantly.

"Sergeant Perl has instructed me to collect you and your belongings and bring you to the base," he said.

The officer was polite and seemed sincere but I was always cautious. I stuck my head out the door and scanned. He was the only one around. An army vehicle sat in the road. It seemed legitimate. I had to trust Sol. I gathered my belongings and thanked Aunt Udel and with that Shoshana and I were off to the military base.

There were approximately four hundred men that had volunteered for the Haganah; the men, along with their families prepared to leave for Palestine. Most of these families were running away from persecution for standing up to the communist movement in some way or another. Many of the wives and families had already settled in at the base by the time that Shoshana and I had arrived.

The Officer brought me up to the small apartment where Sol had been living. I knocked on the door. Before I could even say hello Sol threw his arms around me. It felt wonderful to be a family again. That night at the mess hall he introduced me to many of the families he had made friends with; everyone was excited about the prospect of living in the Holy Land. Everything seemed like things were looking up for us until Shoshana came down with a fever just days before we had to leave.

We visited the military doctor on the base and he gave us penicillin to give to Shoshana. After several days and many dosages, she was still not any better. The doctor assured us that she was not in danger. We boarded a train to Naples, Italy, in the hopes that the doctor was right. The train rocked most passengers to sleep, but my little Shoshana kept coughing, her temperature rose to 105 degrees. I stayed awake with her, keeping her cooled down with ice and cold towels. I prayed that she lived until we made it to Naples.

We arrived in Naples on Christmas Day. Sol and I immediately took Shoshana to the nearest hospital. She was diagnosed with pneumonia. The doctor told us that Shoshana was beyond help and only had a few hours to live. The hospital refused to admit her because we did not have enough money for her care and she was so close to death. Here I was again. I was going to lose my little girl. I held Sol's hand tightly. Tears rolled down my face.

"We have to go," Sol said, pulling me out of the hospital. I knew he was right. There was nothing they could do. My only choice was to hold her tight.

The next part of our journey had us taking a ship to Haifa. We needed to head from the hospital to the dock to make the boat that would take us to Palestine. When we arrived at the ship the captain barred us from boarding because it was illegal to bring a dying person on board. I wasn't going to leave my baby behind.

The ship was ready to sail. I sat on the pier with my dying baby, often bending over to breathe into her mouth when she gasped for air. Sol sat nearby, weeping and broken. It began raining. As the cool rain poured down my face, I realized that staying on the pier and watching my baby die, merely acquiescing to what others judged as inevitable, was unacceptable. *This was not the way I survived and had helped Joli survive the camps.* With renewed resolve, I handed Shoshana to Sol and ran up the gangway past a seaman who tried to bar my way. Frenzied, I looked for the captain. I ran into another man who turned out to be the ship's doctor. I frantically told him my story. I desperately pleaded to the doctor. I searched his face for a hopeful sign. I saw I had gotten through to him. He persuaded the captain to permit my family to board. I had to commit to have Shoshana's body thrown overboard if she died during the trip but I had no intentions of letting her die.

I ran back to Sol and Shoshana. I grabbed his arm.

"Come. We have to hurry. We are getting on the ship," I said.

"I don't understand," he replied.

"You married a survivor," I told him. He grabbed our bags. I took Shoshana in my arms and we ran towards the boat.

Aboard ship, the doctor directly transfused my blood into my child's. And he went further. He convinced the captain on an American aircraft carrier berthed nearby to give him a few doses of streptomycin, a newly discovered drug, to try on my baby. The Italian doctor split the three doses he was given into six. Two days later, Shoshana's temperature began to fall.

Because we were smuggling into the country we needed to be very careful about how we entered. Therefore, when we arrived to the shore of Haifa, the men were armed and taken by small boats to the shore. The infants and children were ferried into Haifa to the men. The next day, the women were allowed off the ship. I found my baby, alive and well with Sol.

EPILOGUE

S OL SERVED IN THE HAGANAH and then the Israeli army for a total of three years. At that time I had enough of the war, bloodshed and fighting. I was ready to exist in a place of peace. All my life, I had dreamed of living in America. I still remembered my Aunt Sylvia's visit and her tales of the opulent and exciting life there. I thought she was the most exotic and beautiful person I had ever seen. We filed the necessary immigration papers for both Canada and America. I wanted to make a fresh start in a New World; when a visa for Canada became available, we seized it. Canada was much closer to the United States than Israel.

Life in Canada was much harder for us than in Israel. We had little money and there was no financial aid from the Canadian government, plus our sponsors were as poor as we were. After three months, Sol was stricken with spinal meningitis and it was a year before he could go out and find a job. To keep us alive, I found a job sewing in a factory. When Sol recovered he became a meat cutter.

My dream still remained to live in America. We applied for a visa, sponsored by one of Sol's cousin. When the visa came through, Sol was reluctant to give up his hard won job for the uncertainties of a new country. We had a long, heated discussion. I just felt this was the right move for us. I also wanted the unborn child I was carrying to be born in the United States. We compromised: if we could not make a go of it in Cleveland, Ohio we would move back to Toronto after the baby was born. In June 1956, we crossed the Canadian border by train into Buffalo, New York. From there, it was just a short trip to Cleveland where our cousins welcomed us. I gave birth to our daughter Debby in November 1956, she was a natural born American citizen. I changed Shoshana's name to Susan, so she too could have an American one.

America proved to be how Aunt Sylvia described it back in 1935 in Vlachovice. My dreams had come true. I changed my name once again to Edith which meant strong, joyful and happy, because I was so very happy.

Each year on the High Holy Days, I remember those who are no longer with me. I remember my Momma, Goldie and the other siblings who were killed during the Holocaust. I remember my Papa who remarried and lived in Israel until his death at the age of 78. I remember my sister Joli and brothers Morci, Moshe and Labji, who have since died after living happy, successful lives with their spouses and children. And, I remember my beloved Sol who died in 1985, far too young. I remember SS Officer Dali, the Hauptstrumfuhrer and the others who helped me as much as they could. I thank God that I had the resolve to survive and to stand up to all those who tried to destroy me.

Seventy years later the nightmares still come but with less frequency. When they come, I fight them away with thoughts of my beloved daughters Susan and Debby; my wonderful son-in-law Chuck, darling grandchildren Stuart and his wife Michelle; Hallie and her husband Ravi; Lindsay and Jackie; and my precious great grandchildren, Isaac, Isabel, Elia, Justice, Lily and Isla.

Every time I read the Kaddish, I give thanks for being alive. And, I give thanks to my Momma for making me promise to survive.

Momma – I have told the story in the hopes that no one will ever forget.

Top Row: Edita, Yidel, Momma, Papa
Bottom Row: Pearl, Mendel, Goldi, Joli
Kalus family photo.
Taken three-years prior to them being seized from their home.

Printed in November 2021
by Rotomail Italia S.p.A., Vignate (MI) - Italy